WILLIAM T. SHERMAN

WILLIAM T. SHERMAN

A Biography

Robert P. Broadwater

GREENWOOD BIOGRAPHIES

⊙ GREENWOOD

AN IMPRINT OF ABC-CLIO, LLC
Santa Barbara, California • Denver, Colorado • Oxford, England

Library of Congress Cataloging-in-Publication Data

Broadwater, Robert P., 1958–
    William T. Sherman : a biography / Robert P. Broadwater.
        pages cm. — (Greenwood biographies)
    Includes bibliographical references and index.
    ISBN 978-1-4408-0060-3 (hardcopy : alk. paper) — ISBN 978-1-4408-0061-0
(ebook) 1. Sherman, William T. (William Tecumseh), 1820–1891. 2. United
States—History—Civil War, 1861–1865—Biography. 3. Generals—United
States—Biography. 4. United States. Army—Biography. I. Title.
    E467.1.S55B86 2013
    355.092—dc23 [B]   2012047690

ISBN: 978-1-4408-0060-3
EISBN: 978-1-4408-0061-0

17 16 15 14 13   1 2 3 4 5

This book is also available on the World Wide Web as an eBook.
Visit www.abc-clio.com for details.

Greenwood
An Imprint of ABC-CLIO, LLC

ABC-CLIO, LLC
130 Cremona Drive, P.O. Box 1911
Santa Barbara, California 93116-1911

This book is printed on acid-free paper ∞

Manufactured in the United States of America

CONTENTS

SERIES FOREWORD

In response to school and library needs, ABC-CLIO publishes this distinguished series of full-length biographies specifically for student use. Prepared by field experts and professionals, these engaging biographies are tailored for students who need challenging yet accessible biographies. Ideal for school assignments and student research, the length, format, and subject areas are designed to meet educators' requirements and students' interests.

ABC-CLIO offers an extensive selection of biographies spanning all curriculum-related subject areas including social studies, the sciences, literature and the arts, history and politics, and popular culture, covering public figures and famous personalities from all time periods and backgrounds, both historic and contemporary, who have made an impact on American and/or world culture. The subjects of these biographies were chosen based on comprehensive feedback from librarians and educators. Consideration was given to both curriculum relevance and inherent interest. Readers will find a wide array of subject choices from fascinating entertainers like Miley Cyrus and Lady Gaga to inspiring leaders like John F. Kennedy and Nelson Mandela, from the greatest athletes of our time like Michael Jordan and Muhammad Ali, to the most amazing success stories of our day like J. K. Rowling and Oprah.

While the emphasis is on fact, not glorification, the books are meant to be fun to read. Each volume provides in-depth information about the subject's life from birth through childhood, the teen years, and adulthood. A thorough account relates family background and education, traces personal and professional influences, and explores struggles, accomplishments, and contributions. A timeline highlights the most significant life events against an historical perspective. Bibliographies supplement the reference value of each volume.

PREFACE

William Tecumseh Sherman forged a military reputation in the Civil War that catapulted him to national fame and worldwide acclaim. He is both hailed and criticized for his military strategies and the era of modern total warfare they ushered in. His capture of Atlanta and March to the Sea brought the South to its knees and was instrumental in securing the final victory for the Union. By the end of the war, Sherman was regarded as one of the greatest generals in American military history, a substantial change in fortunes for an officer who had been relieved of command in Kentucky in 1861 due to a nervous breakdown brought about by the strain of responsibility. A complex and controversial individual, Sherman's life seems to be a contradiction in many respects. Although he was almost universally held to be a villain in the South because of his scorched-earth treatment of Georgia and the Carolinas, he was honored by the residents of Baton Rouge, Louisiana, where his portrait hung at the Louisiana State Seminary of Learning & Military Academy for the duration of the war. This scourge of the South nearly ended his military career in shame because the terms he gave to a surrendering Confederate army were so lenient that his political superiors in Washington considered them to be treasonous. His wartime actions ensured freedom for the slaves, but he refused to have any black soldiers serve with his army. Sherman held politics and politicians in complete disdain, even though his own brother served in Congress, and his military career was advanced due to political alliances. In the wars against the Plains Indians, Sherman adopted the philosophy that "the only good Indian is a dead Indian," while at the same time becoming an advocate for the fair and humane treatment of those Indians residing on reservations. His death was also a source of irony and contradiction. General Joseph E. Johnston, his greatest nemesis during the Civil War, attended the funeral of his old foe, contracting a case of pneumonia that would claim his life because he insisted on paying his respects by standing bareheaded in the bitterly cold February weather. Even his name was a source of controversy. Sherman was nine years old when his father died and he was sent to live with a foster family. His foster mother stated that his name at this time was simply Tecumseh Sherman, and that he acquired the first name of William when he was baptized by a Dominican priest. In his memoirs, Sherman states that his father had given him the name William Tecumseh when he was an infant, and that he was baptized with that name by a Presbyterian minister when he was a baby. Although his son, Thomas, became a Catholic priest, Sherman himself adhered to no organized religion.

In a military career that spanned more than four decades, Sherman ascended to the top of his profession, becoming commanding general of the U.S. Army. His fame was worldwide, and his campaigns would be studied by generations of military students around the globe. Military historian Sir Basil Liddell Hart proclaimed him to be the "first modern general," and one of the most important strategists in the annals of war, stating that he was an equal to Napoleon Bonaparte. Sherman's strategy and tactics contributed heavily to the mechanized warfare adopted by the Germans in World War II, known as Blitzkrieg. He also influenced General George S. Patton, who had studied his campaigns and conducted his own sweep across Europe in what he called "super-Sherman style."

Raised in an age of chivalry and romantic notions about the glory of war, Sherman emerges as a voice of truth and stark reality. He viewed war to be neither chivalrous nor glorious. "War is cruelty, and you cannot refine it," he wrote. Even in this there is contradiction. Sherman's goal was to win the war and end the killing as soon as possible. To achieve this objective, he waged war against not just enemy armies, but civilian populations, as well. He destroyed not only military installations and goods, but also civilian property and private homes. The city of Atlanta was put to the torch, and a 60-mile swath of charred devastation marked his march across Georgia in the name of humanely bringing the bloody conflict to a close through the use of inhumane methods. His campaigns made him a hero-god to the North and a villain of mythical proportion to the South. The bottom line is that William T. Sherman had an aptitude and appetite for war, and was first, last, and always a soldier. He approached war for what it was: a gruesome tragedy that can only be ended by being victorious or vanquished, and he sought to bring the nightmare to its conclusion in the speediest manner possible.

Memoirs of General W.T. Sherman, Written By Himself, volumes I and II, published by D. Appleton & Company in 1875, has been relied upon heavily in the writing of this biography. Sherman has been described as being gifted in his ability to express himself, and Mark Twain thought that he was a master of narrative writing. As such, his memoirs provide not only historical facts, but also insights to the emotions and motivations of the man. Additional insight is provided through biographical works such as *Sherman and His Campaigns: A Military Biography*, written by Colonel S.M. Bowman and Lt. Col. R.B. Irwin, and published by Charles B. Richardson in 1865; *The Life of General William T. Sherman*, written by James P Boyd, and published by Publisher's Union in 1891; *Life and Deeds of General Sherman*, written by Henry Davenport Northrop, and published by Pennsylvania Publishing Co. in 1891, and *Sherman: Fighting Prophet*, written by Lloyd Lewis, and published by Harcourt, Brace and Company in 1932. A more complete disclosure of the sources used in writing this book is included in the bibliographical essay at the end of this work.

The purpose of this book is to provide the reader with a balanced and factual biography of this famous military leader of the Civil War, a man who helped to shape the nation's history. It is not the intention of the writer to eulogize or pay tribute to the subject, but rather to provide a fair and objective narrative that factually chronicles the complete story of his life. In the process, it is hoped that William Tecumseh Sherman may be brought to life for the reader, and that this complex man of war may be viewed for what he was: a professional soldier who was good at his craft.

TIMELINE: EVENTS IN THE LIFE OF WILLIAM T. SHERMAN

February 8, 1820	Born in Lancaster, Ohio.
June 24, 1829	Charles Sherman dies.
May 20, 1836	Sherman leaves Lancaster en route for West Point.
July 1, 1836	Begins education at West Point.
June 1840	Graduates West Point, assigned as a second lieutenant in the Second U.S. Artillery.
October 1840	Reports for duty against the Seminole in Florida.
November 30, 1841	Promoted to first lieutenant and transferred to St. Augustine.
February 1842	Transferred to Fort Morgan at Mobile, Alabama.
June 1842	Transferred to Fort Moultrie in Charleston.
May 1846	Assigned to recruiting duty in Pittsburgh, Pennsylvania.
July 14, 1846	Sails from New York aboard the *Lexington* for California.
January 26, 1847	Arrives safely in Monterrey, California.

February 2, 1848	Treaty of Guadalupe Hidalgo ends the Mexican American War.
September 27, 1850	Marries Ellen Ewing.
	Promoted to the rank of captain.
January 18, 1851	Maria Ewing Sherman is born.
March 17, 1852	Mary Elizabeth Sherman is born.
September 6, 1853	Resigns his commission in the army.
October 15, 1853	Arrives in San Francisco to take over Lucas, Turner & Co.
June 8, 1854	William Tecumseh Sherman Jr. is born.
June 2, 1856	Is ordered to turn out the California Militia against vigilantes.
October 12, 1856	Thomas Ewing Sherman is born.
May 1, 1857	Leaves California.
January 30, 1858	Dissolves the firm of Lucas, Turner & Co.
January 1, 1859	The firm of Sherman, Ewing & McCook is established.
September 5, 1859	Eleanor Mary Sherman is born.
November 1859	Appointed superintendent of the Louisiana Military Academy.
May 11, 1860	Caught in the St. Louis Riot.
November 6, 1860	Abraham Lincoln is elected president of the United States.
February 19, 1861	Sherman resigns and leaves Louisiana Military Academy.
May 14, 1861	Appointed colonel of the 13th U.S. Infantry.
July 5, 1861	Rachael Ewing Sherman is born.
July 21, 1861	Battle of Bull Run, or Manassas.
August 7, 1861	Promoted to brigadier general of volunteers.
October 5, 1861	Assigned to command of the Department of the Cumberland.
November 12, 1861	Relieved of command of the Department of the Cumberland.
April 6–7, 1862	Fights in the battle of Shiloh.

Note: In the printed timeline, "May 1, 1850 — Marries Ellen Ewing." appears before "September 27, 1850 — Promoted to the rank of captain."

May 1, 1862	Promoted to the rank of major general of volunteers.
July 21, 1862	Arrives in Memphis, Tennessee, to assume military command of the city.
December 2, 1862	Leads expedition that initiates the Vicksburg campaign.
December 26–29, 1862	Battle of Chickasaw Bluffs.
January 4, 1863	Appointed to command of the XV Corps.
April 30–May 1, 1863	Engagement at Haines's Bluff.
May 14, 1863	Jackson, Mississippi, is captured.
May 19, 1863	First assault on Vicksburg.
May 22, 1863	Second assault on Vicksburg.
July 4, 1863	General Pemberton surrenders his army and Vicksburg is captured.
July 17, 1863	Jackson, Mississippi, is captured by forces under Sherman.
October 3, 1863	William T. Sherman Jr. dies in Memphis of typhoid fever.
October 11, 1863	Engagement at Collierville, Tennessee.
November 24, 1863	Battle of Lookout Mountain.
November 25, 1863	Battle of Missionary Ridge.
May 5, 1864	The Atlanta Campaign commences.
May 7–9, 1864	Engagement at Rocky Face Ridge, Georgia.
May 25, 1864	Battle of New Hope Church.
June 11, 1864	Charles Celestine Sherman is born.
June 27, 1864	Battle of Kennesaw Mountain.
July 20, 1864	Battle of Peach Tree Creek.
July 22, 1864	Battle of Atlanta.
July 28, 1864	Battle of Ezra Church.
August 31, 1864	Battle of Jonesboro.
September 2, 1864	Capture of Atlanta.
November 15, 1864	March to the Sea begins.
November 22, 1864	Battle of Griswoldville, Georgia.
November 23, 1864	Milledgeville, Georgia, is captured.
November 28, 1864	Battle of Buck Head Creek.
November 30, 1864	Battle of Honey Hill, South Carolina.

December 10, 1864	Sherman arrives at Savannah.
December 21, 1864	Savannah is captured by Federal troops.
February 1, 1865	The march through the Carolinas begins.
February 3, 1865	Engagement at River's Bridge, South Carolina.
February 17, 1865	Capture of Columbia, South Carolina.
March 7, 1865	Battle of Kinston, North Carolina.
March 10, 1865	Battle of Monroe's Crossroads, North Carolina.
March 11, 1865	Capture of Fayetteville, North Carolina.
March 19–21, 1865	Battle of Bentonville.
April 26, 1865	Surrender of General Johnston's army at Bennett Place.
May 24, 1865	Grand Review of the western armies in Washington.
May 30, 1865	Sherman takes his leave of the army.
June 27, 1865	Appointed to command of the Military Division of the Mississippi.
July 25, 1865	Promoted to the rank of lieutenant general.
January 9, 1867	Philemon Tecumseh Sherman is born.
March 4, 1869	Promoted to the rank of full general and appointed general of the army.
September 7, 1869	Appointed interim secretary of war.
November 1871	Begins a 10-month tour of Europe.
November 1, 1883	Resigns as general of the army.
February 8, 1884	Retires from the army.
June 5, 1884	Rejects the nomination of the Republican Party as presidential candidate.
November 28, 1888	Ellen Sherman dies in New York City.
February 14, 1891	William T. Sherman dies in New York City.

Chapter 1

ANCESTORS, LINEAGE, AND EARLY YEARS

William Tecumseh Sherman was born on February 8, 1820, in Lancaster, Ohio, as the second son of Charles Robert Sherman and Mary Hoyt Sherman. Charles Sherman forged a life for himself in the legal profession, being admitted to the Ohio Bar in 1809, the sixth generation of Shermans to become a lawyer. His private practice and reputation were so great that Charles became an Ohio Supreme Court judge in 1823. The War of 1812 forced Sherman to take an interlude from his legal practice, becoming a major in the Ohio Militia in the war against England. In 1813, the Ohio frontier was secured when the British and their Shawnee allies were defeated at the Battle of the Thames, in Canada. The great Shawnee chief, Tecumseh, was killed in this battle. Tecumseh was respected and admired by Americans for the way he conducted himself with encroaching settlers, and Charles Sherman was so taken with the chief that he named one of his sons in his honor. For Charles Sherman, military service was the obligation of a free man to defend liberty against tyrannical oppression. He was a citizen soldier in every respect, a civilian, called to duty in time of need, who returned to civilian life as soon as the crisis had passed. For his son, William, the military would not be an obligation, but a chosen profession and a way of life.

Drawing of the house Sherman was born in at Lancaster, Ohio. (U.S. Army Military History Institute)

The Sherman family was of English descent, and the branch on which William Tecumseh traced his lineage had been rooted in America for almost two centuries by the time of his birth. Edmund Sherman is shown on the public records of Massachusetts to have been a resident of that colony before 1636, most probably arriving in America in 1634. Edmund moved to the Connecticut Valley, where he became a leading citizen of the Connecticut Colony. Edmund's son, Samuel, also born in England, assumed his father's role of leadership within the colony, as did his son, John, born in 1651, and his grandson, John Jr., born in 1687. John Sherman Jr.'s son, Daniel, born in 1721, would continue the fifth generation of leadership in Connecticut and would become a patriot in the cause of independence during the Revolutionary War. Daniel's son, Taylor, was born in 1758 and would be a young man by the time the war with England was ended. His son, Charles Robert Sherman, would be born as an American citizen, not a subject of the crown, in September of 1788.

Charles Sherman had established himself as a noted juror, and in 1813 President James Madison appointed him Collector of Internal

Revenue for the Third Ohio District, embracing six counties around Lancaster. It had been the custom for local bank notes to be accepted as payment for taxes, but in 1817, the Federal government announced that only gold or U.S. Bank Notes would be accepted. Sherman's deputy collectors had all accepted local bank notes to pay the taxes in the district, and, as these were no longer honored by the national government, Sherman's ledgers showed a huge deficiency. Sherman believed it was his sole responsibility to make good for the shortfall. He gave all of his money as a down payment on the debt, making payments on the balance for the remainder of his life. This act of honor caused the Sherman family to be listed among the poorer residents of Lancaster, though Charles was a well-respected and influential member of the community.

Charles was riding his circuit route, presiding over court cases, in June of 1829, when he arrived in Lebanon. After taking sick in the courtroom, he died six days later, on June 24. Charles's death left the Sherman family destitute. His debt of honor to the government had exhausted his financial resources, and his death left his widow and their 11 children with no means of support. The Sherman family may have been poor in finances, but it was rich in the support of family and friends. The family was broken up, as the children were sent to live with different families. Nine-year-old William Tecumseh was sent to the home of Thomas and Maria Ewing. It was said that Thomas Ewing approached Sherman's mother after Charles had died, pointing out the fact that she had many mouths to feed, and offering to take one of the children into his own home. He stated that he wished to take the brightest and most promising under his care, and Elizabeth, Sherman's 17-year-old sister, proclaimed William to be the brightest and most promising of her siblings. Ewing accepted the girl's judgment, took the boy in tow, and made him his son. Sherman would later write that Judge Ewing "ever after treated me as his own son." Thomas Ewing, an attorney, was an influential member of the Whig Party, who would serve as a U.S. Senator and the first U.S. Secretary of the Interior. He was a close, personal friend of Charles Sherman, and the families had been tied together since the time Charles first arrived in Lancaster. The Ewings already had three children of their own, and Maria would give birth to a fourth in August of that year. Over the coming years, two more siblings would be born to the family, and William Tecumseh, or Cump, as he was usually called by his family and friends, would find himself part of a foster family almost as large as his natural one. Over the coming years, Thomas Ewing would have reason to agree with Elizabeth's estimation that young William was the most promising of her siblings. In later years he would recall, "There was nothing specially remarkable about him excepting that I never knew so young a boy who could do an errand so correctly and promptly as he did. He was transparently honest, faithful and reliable. Studious and correct in his habits, his progress in education was steady and substantial."

There is some controversy connected to Sherman's name at the time he went to live with the Ewings. According to one account, his given name, at this time, was simply Tecumseh. Maria Ewing, a devout Catholic, had the boy baptized by a Dominican priest, and it was at this time that he acquired the first name of William. Sherman disputes this account in his Memoirs, stating that his father had given him the name William Tecumseh, and that he had been baptized with that name while still an infant. He had gotten the nickname of Cump because some of his younger brothers and sisters had trouble pronouncing Tecumseh. For the remainder of his life, Cump would be the name he was called by those closest to him.

By all accounts, the Ewings provided Sherman with a loving and nurturing home, and the boy was readily accepted by his foster brothers and sisters. It was also helpful that the Ewings lived in Lancaster, and Sherman did not have to be uprooted to live in strange surroundings. In fact, the brick home of the Ewings was a mere half block away from the frame structure Cump had called home for the first nine years of his life. This was the home and family he was well acquainted with. The Ewing's and Sherman's children had grown up together and had spent endless amount of time at each other's homes. Philemon Ewing was Sherman's best friend, constant companion, and more brother than neighbor. In a way, it was as if he had gained an extended family. Sherman still had regular contact with his natural mother and siblings, as he grew accustomed to his new surroundings. Young Cump was also fortunate in that the Ewings were able to offer him certain advantages because of the resources and influence the family possessed. The second half of his childhood would be spent in an atmosphere of comfortable plenty, where his wants and needs would be cared for. Sherman would live with the Ewings for seven years, but the bond of love and respect he formed would last till the end of his life.

Sherman's life in Lancaster was much the same as any other boy growing up in that small town. In fact, the only thing that distinguished him from other boys of his own age were the flaming red locks of hair on his head. His educational instruction took place at the Lancaster Academy, a private school that had been established in the town in 1820, supplanting the log-house institution that had previously been used. Charles Sherman and Thomas Ewing had been instrumental in establishing the school and were two of its greatest supporters, financially. In 1825, Mark and Samuel Howe assumed administration of the school. The Howes, an enlightened pair of brothers, taught an extensive course of studies. Students were instructed in the three Rs, as well as Latin, Greek, and French. All in all, the education Sherman received at the Lancaster Academy was the equal of any instruction he could have received in an eastern school. As an adult, Sherman would state that the Lancaster Academy was as fine an institution of learning as was to be found anywhere in Ohio. Although never the top student in his class, Cump showed a capacity for learning that must have gratified the Ewings.

Sherman spent his time outside the schoolhouse engaged in activities that occupied the attention of all young boys of the era. Hunting was good in the woods surrounding Lancaster, and many hours were passed in this way. A local pond was a favorite gathering place for the children of the town. Swimming helped to cool the hot summer days, and skating provided exercise and fellowship in the winter. Horseback riding and playing soldier would surely have been among the boy's activities. As with most boys, Cump was not immune to acts of youthful exuberance that turned out badly. Ashamed of his red hair, he once determined to alter the color. Gathering an assortment of medicines, drugs, and lotions, he concocted a potion he was sure would dye his hair to a more acceptable shade of brown. When he used the concoction, however, it turned his hair into an interesting shade of green. The color would not wash out and had to be endured until his hair grew out again. From that time onward, Sherman showed little concern for his outward appearance.

Throughout the year, there was a constant stream of interesting and influential people stopping by to pay respects to the Ewing family. Among these, Thomas Corwin seems to have made the greatest impression on Cump. Corwin was an influential member of the Whig Party. He had served in the Ohio House of Representatives, and, in 1830, was elected to the U.S. House of Representatives. He later served as governor of Ohio and as a U.S. Senator from Ohio. Corwin was an excellent orator and storyteller. Westerners were known for the ability to tell tall tales, and men like Daniel Boone and Davy Crockett became national celebrities due to the oral history relayed by these westerners. Corwin was as adept in this sort of western oratory as any of his rival politicians, and his speeches were delivered with earthy wisdom and home-spun humor. Corwin spoke rapidly and endlessly, and young Cump hung on every word. This man was more than an entertaining visitor. Corwin had been a close personal friend of Cump's father and had been with Charles Sherman when he died. He represented a bond with Cump's beloved father, and it was easy for the boy to form a strong admiration for him. Young Sherman paid homage to Corwin by emulating his style of speaking. As he grew, he gained a reputation for speaking rapidly and endlessly, seeded with the same sort of humor and logic that had become Corwin's trademark.

With a mind that easily grasped abstract theories and an intellect that readily absorbed new information, Sherman nonetheless enjoyed working with his hands. During his days at West Point, when thinking about his coming graduation, he once confided that he would prefer to earn his living as a blacksmith. In 1834, at the age of 14, Cump had his first opportunity to make his own way through physical labor, and he found that he enjoyed it. That summer, a new canal was being dug from nearby Carroll, Ohio to the Ohio River, via Athens, Ohio. Cump was numbered among a group of boys selected from the town to work on the project. He was already considered to be large and strong for his age, and that summer, spent in vigorous work as a rodman, only served to enhance his physique. In addition, he was paid one silver 50-cent piece for each day of work, a substantial wage when most working men made less than 10 dollars per month. Sherman worked on the canal during the fall of 1834 and the spring of 1835. It was the first wages he had ever earned. For several years now, he had been housed, clothed, and fed through the charity of others, and the feeling of self-reliance at earning his own way must have been liberating to him. He also found that hard physical labor agreed with him.

In 1835, Cump turned 15, and Judge Ewing determined that the time had come to look to the boy's future. Accordingly, he decided that an appointment to the U.S. Military Academy, at West Point, would be a suitable answer. Cump would have an opportunity to further his education at the academy, as well as the prospect of making his living as an officer in the army.

As Sherman passed from boyhood into adolescence, he experienced his first encounter with romance. For Cump, it could be said that the object of his affection was a childhood sweetheart, and he did not have to look far for the source of his infatuation. Eleanor Ewing, his foster sister, was the object of his passion. Four years his junior, the two had grown up together. As time passed, they had gone from being playmates to becoming soul mates, however. As Cump grew into adolescence, he became solicitous toward Ellen, and to her he displayed his most chivalrous and gentlemanly behavior. Philemon was still his best friend, but Ellen had become his confidant and the person who best understood his thoughts and actions. The two shared the intimacies of their hopes and dreams, found joy in each other's successes, and comforted one another in times of tribulation

In the spring of 1836, Sherman received his appointment to West Point, through his foster father, Thomas Ewing. He would soon be taking leave of his second family to make his way in the world. The Ewings had become more than benefactors to him. Indeed, his love for them equaled that which he felt for his natural family, and it was with a heavy heart that he bid them farewell. The adieu that he bade to Ellen was the hardest of all. He promised to write often and to tell her everything taking place in his life. In this, he was as good as his word, for the letters he wrote to Ellen while a cadet at West Point revealed thoughts and feelings he entrusted to no other living soul.

Chapter 2

WEST POINT DAYS

Cump departed Lancaster, traveling by stagecoach to Zanesville. From there, he made his way on the National Highway, present day Route 40, to Frederick, Maryland. He was supposed to take the train from Frederick to Washington, but he opted to continue on by coach, owing to the fact that he was wary of riding on the newly fangled iron contraptions. Upon arriving in Washington, Sherman made his way to the boarding house Senator Ewing rented for a reunion with his foster-father. A full week was spent in the city, seeing the sites and meeting influential people. Cump spent a full hour spying on President Andrew Jackson through the fence that surrounded the White House, gazing in awe as Old Hickory paced back and forth on the lawn of the executive mansion. Martin Van Buren, Henry Clay, John C. Calhoun, Daniel Webster, and Lewis Cass were among the distinguished members of the government that Sherman had the opportunity to meet in person. The wonders of the capital must have seemed grand to the young lad from Ohio.

With his vacation in Washington concluded, he bade farewell to Senator Ewing and, overcoming his fears, boarded a train for Baltimore. From there, he took a boat to Havre de Grace, where he again boarded a train for Wilmington, Delaware. From Wilmington, he caught another boat to Philadelphia and eventually made his way to New York City, where he spent a week visiting relatives living in the city. From New York, he boarded a final boat for the last leg of his journey, up the Hudson River, to West Point.

William Tecumseh Sherman was officially entered upon the roll of cadets at West Point on July 1, 1836. Over the next four years, he would not only gain instruction in all the courses deemed necessary to becoming an efficient officer in the U.S. Army, but he would also make the acquaintance of many of the men who would serve as officers in the Union and Confederate armies during the Civil War. Twelve members of his own class would go on to become generals in that war, including George H. Thomas, Richard S. Ewell, and Bushrod Johnson. He would also come to know promising cadets in other classes coming into the academy as junior-classmen during his time at West Point. In all, he would make the acquaintance of some 65 future Union and Confederate generals during his time at the academy, including such notables as: James P. Longstreet, Ulysses S. Grant, Daniel Harvey Hill, Don Carlos Buell, Earl Van Dorn, Lafayette McLaws, Abner Doubleday, William S. Rosecrans, John Pope, and William B. Franklin. Cump would command, or serve under, many of these men during the Civil War, and he would also fight against a large number of them. The invaluable insight into the character and abilities of these men that he gained at the academy would serve him well in later years, but for now, they were all fellow cadets, doing the best they could to master the course work laid before them, and trying not to amass too many demerits.

Sherman was a capable student, and his educational foundation proved to be more than sufficient to stand him in good stead, academically, as he placed near the top of his class in all courses of instruction. Military bearing was another matter. Sherman's appearance was usually unkempt, and his attention to the finer points of military courtesy left something to be desired. He later remembered that "At the Academy I was not considered a good soldier. . . . Then, as now, neatness in dress and form, with a strict conformity to the rules, were the qualifications required for office."

Sherman had been assigned to the Old South Barracks, and among his roommates were George H. Thomas and Stewart Van Vliet.

Van Vliet left a written reminiscence of how the trio formed a lasting friendship during their time spent together at West Point: "Sherman, George H. Thomas and I arrived at West Point on the same day, and all three were assigned to the same room on the south side of the old south barracks. A warm friendship commenced in that room, which continued, without a single break, during our lives. We were all three sturdy fellows, which prevented our being annoyed by the older cadets. They commenced to haze us, as was the fashion of those days, but Thomas put a stop to it. One evening a cadet came into our room and commenced to give us orders. He had said but a few words when Old Tom, as we always called him, stepped up to him and said 'Leave this room immediately, or I will throw you through the window.' It is needless to say that the cadet lost no time in getting out of the room. There were no more attempts to haze us." From this glimpse, it may seem as if Cump and his companions had formed a clique among themselves, for self-preservation, and that his time at West Point might have been spent in an adversarial relationship with the upperclassmen. Nothing could be further from the truth. Upperclassmen admired plebes who stood up for themselves, and Sherman, Thomas, and Van Vliet scored high marks among the vast majority of their superiors for not backing down to the cadet that had come to haze them.

The first year of instruction at the academy was a grueling combination of French, algebra, trigonometry, ministration of planes and solids, and the school of the soldier. The sophomore year consisted of French rhetoric, geography, history, and artillery. The summer after the sophomore year was a time to be longed for by all cadets, for it was at that time that they received their first furlough to go home and visit their families. A two-month period was allotted for this purpose, and it was commonly the first time the cadet had seen family and loved ones since arriving at West Point. Sherman spent his entire furlough at home in Ohio, visiting with the Ewings and his natural family. Following this much needed respite, it was time to report to the academy for the junior year of instruction. Courses that year consisted of drawing, natural philosophy, chemistry, the school of the battalion, and another artillery course. The senior year curriculum was supremely challenging and was made up of engineering, science of war, mineralogy and geology, moral philosophy, political science, rhetoric, and a final installment of artillery training.

As the spring of 1840 gave way to summer, Cump prepared himself for graduation from West Point and assuming his place as an officer in the U.S. Army. More than 100 cadets had reported to the banks of the Hudson River to be admitted to the academy in the summer of 1836. Of that number, only 42 yet remained. Sherman's academic record placed him fourth in his class standing, but the effects of his demerits lowered him to a final standing of sixth. Senator Ewing had hoped that Cump would be assigned to the Corps of Engineers, following his commission, but this honor was reserved for the top graduates, and Sherman's standing fell just short of the requirements. Cump had written to Ellen that he intended to spend only a year in the service before resigning his commission to follow his father's footsteps and study law. But as graduation neared, he experienced a change of heart. "Indeed, the nearer we come to that dreadful epoch, graduation day, the higher opinion I conceive of the duties and life of an officer of the United States Army, and the more confirmed in the wish of spending my life in the service of my country."

Instead of a coveted appointment to the Corps of Engineers, Sherman was posted as a Second lieutenant in the Third U.S. Artillery, stationed in Florida, and taking part in the war against the Seminole Indians. As with most young officers, Sherman was pleased with the assignment. Promotion in the army was extremely slow, unless one had the opportunity to distinguish himself on the field of battle. The chance to prove your mettle against a hostile foe is the most that any professional soldier can ask for, so Sherman viewed his posting with a certain amount of gratification. It had been two years since he had seen his family, however, and first things came first. It was customary that another furlough was granted to cadets upon, graduation, before they were due to report for duty with their regiment. Sherman availed himself of another extended visit, in Lancaster, with his natural and extended family, and the summer of 1840 was spent in blissful contact with those he loved. In October of that year, he reported for duty in Florida. When bidding farewell to his family, it must have served as some sort of consolation to know that his arrival in Florida would place him in contact again with one of his closest adult friends.

George Thomas and Stewart Van Vliet, his roommates from West Point, had also been assigned as new lieutenants to the Third U.S. Artillery. At least there would be trusted and friendly faces to greet him when he arrived in Florida, but that did not diminish the sorrow he felt at taking his leave from Ellen, with no idea when he would see her again.

Chapter 3

DUTY IN FLORIDA

In September 1840, Cump began the journey to Florida. He first reported to Governor's Island, in New York Harbor, where he was assigned a command position in a company of raw recruits enlisted in the Third U.S. Artillery. Nearly a month was spent training the volunteers as artillerists before orders arrived directing Sherman's company, now designated Company A, to make its way to Savannah, Georgia. Van Vliet had also been assigned to Company A, whereas Thomas was posted to Company D. The troops boarded a ship that took them to their assigned point, and from there they were ferried to Florida. Cump's company was posted at Fort Pierce, along the Indian River. Company D was stationed at Fort Lauderdale, so Sherman and Van Vliet had to bid a temporary adieu to Thomas.

When Sherman arrived in Florida, there were no offensive operations taking place, and his first month was spent getting acclimated to his new surroundings. Fishing and hunting occupied many of his leisure hours, providing variety to the boring rations issued by the army. Green turtles were in abundance in the area and became regular fare at the officers' mess, so much so that the soldiers tired of them and preferred to go back to the salt–beef ration. Sherman did not just hunt

Lt. William T. Sherman as he appeared following his graduation from West Point. (U.S. Military History Institute)

wildlife for meat, but he also sought out animal companions to occupy his time. Indeed, judging from one letter he wrote, his quarters had become something of a zoo. He had gotten several chickens and "a little fawn to play with, and crows, a crane, etc., and if you were to enter my room you would doubt whether it was the abode of man or beasts. In one corner is a hen, setting; in another , some crows, roosted on bushes; the other is a little bed of bushes for the little fawn; whilst in the fourth is my bucket, washbasin, glass, etc. . . . I have yet more pets than any bachelor in the country-innumerable chickens, tame pigeons, white rabbits and a full-blooded Indian pony." Cump enjoyed taking care of the animals, and explained that his time was better spent in this way "than in drinking or gambling."

In November 1840, offensive operations against the Indians were resumed. These consisted chiefly of detachments being sent by boat to round up any Seminole that could be found and take them prisoner. All such captives were then sent to the Oklahoma Territory for resettlement. The winter progressed in this fashion. There were no battles and precious few armed encounters with the enemy. It was more police work than soldiering, and there was little glory to be gained in rounding up stragglers, or those too old, weak, or infirm to keep up with the rest of the tribe. To Cump, it must have seemed as if the chance to distinguish himself and earn promotion would never come in the swamps of Florida.

During the summer of 1841, an incident took place that brought Sherman to the attention of his superiors. A number of Seminoles came to Fort Pierce, accompanied by a black man named Joe who spoke English. Joe explained that the Seminole chief, Coacoochee, or Wild Cat, was nearby and wished to hold a council at the post. Joe handed over a pass issued by Brigadier General William J. Worth, commander of the army in Florida. Major Thomas Childs, commander of Fort Pierce, agreed to the meeting with the chief and sent Sherman and a party of mounted troops along with Joe and the Indians to escort Coacoochee to the fort. When the chief arrived, he told Major Childs that he was tired of fighting. He wanted to end the war and the suffering of his people. Coacoochee said that he and his people were willing to relocate to reservations, in Oklahoma Territory, and asked for a month of rations for his tribe while they prepared to do so. Major Childs agreed to this, at which time liquor somehow appeared, and the chief proceeded to get unceremoniously drunk. When Coacoochee sobered up, a few days later, he took the rations and made his way back into the Everglades. But the promised delivery of his people to the fort did not take place. Every few day, the chief would send a message requesting more provisions and asking for more whiskey, but there was no word as to when the arrival of his people could be expected. At the end of the month, Major Childs surmised that he had been duped, and that Coacoochee had tricked him into providing supplies for his people.

Childs sent word to Coacoochee requesting another council be held. The chief accepted and arrived at the fort with a party of braves. A quantity of whiskey was produced and all of the Indians became drunk and passed out. Sherman, Van Vliet, and several other men then shackled the entire party in irons, and when they sobered up, it was to be sent to Oklahoma, as prisoners. Sherman was cited in the official report of the capture of Chief Coacoochee, and it was his first such recognition for accomplishment in the service. Capturing drunken prisoners was not exactly the sort of action Cump had in mind when he arrived in Florida, but the elimination of Chief Coacoochee was viewed by his superiors as a major success in the war against the Seminole.

On November 30, 1841, Sherman was promoted to first lieutenant and transferred to Company G, in St. Augustine, Florida. It was his first promotion, and the part he played in the capture of Coacoochee was a prime reason for the distinction. St. Augustine was a little closer to civilization than Fort Pierce, and the living conditions were much improved, but Cump was not thrilled with the assignment. What he really wanted was a transfer to duty on the western frontier. In a letter to Senator Ewing, he broached the subject. "We hear that the new Secretary of War intends proposing to the next Congress to raise two rifle regiments for Western service. As you are in Washington I presume you can learn whether it is so or not, for I should like to go in such a regiment, if stationed in the Far West." Nothing came of his inquiry about a western regiment, but in February 1842, Sherman was transferred to Fort Morgan, in Mobile, Alabama. He performed garrison duty there until June, when he was ordered to report to Charleston, South Carolina, where he would be stationed at Fort Moultrie.

In the antebellum South, the uniform of a young army officer was enough to open many doors. Because of the fact that his foster father was a respected leader of the Whig Party, Cump was welcomed into the best society circles in Charleston. His service was strictly confined to garrison duty at Fort Moultrie, enabling him to have ample leisure time. Hunting and fishing were common pastimes, but the majority of his off-duty hours were spent mingling with the finest families of the city. Sherman cultivated numerous friendships among Charleston's gentry. Cump truly liked these Southerners. He respected their cultured manners, enjoyed their leisurely lifestyle, thrilled in their educated and intellectual conversations, and availed himself of the plenty that seemed to be everywhere within this circle of new found friends. Indeed, the invitations to social events were so numerous that Cump, and other officers, had to develop a system of rotation for attending them. "These parties are very various," Sherman said, "from the highly aristocratic and fashionable, with sword and epaulettes, or horse-racing, picnicking, boating, fishing, swimming, and God knows what not." Back in Lancaster, he had been accustomed to being looked upon as being affluent, because of the resources and influence of the Ewings, but these new friends far eclipsed the social and financial status he had known in Ohio. It was all so grand and exciting, and Sherman decided that he liked Southern people and the Southern lifestyle very much. He could never conceive, at that time, that his future actions would be as influential as any other act in bringing about the demise of the Southern way of life.

During the summer of 1843, Cump received a three-month pass, which he used to go home to Lancaster. Charleston society may have turned his head, but no Southern belle had laid claim to his attentions. Ellen Ewing was still the object of his affections, and he blissfully spent his prolonged leave with her. When the time came to return to Charleston, Sherman made a roundabout return trip, going by way of New Orleans. First, he made a stop at Cincinnati, where he paid a visit to his two brothers. Next, he went to St. Louis, where he spent a week at Jefferson Barracks. Cump was impressed by both the city and the barracks. At that time, St. Louis was a growing concern of some 40,000 citizens, and Jefferson Barracks was the largest military installation in the United States. The hustle and bustle of this sprawling city, combined with the martial grandeur of Jefferson Barracks must have intensified Cump's desire to receive a transfer to a regiment detailed to this region.

Upon his return to Charleston, Sherman showed an interest in improving his mind. He did a great deal of reading, focusing on classic works, as well as law books. "I have no idea of making the law a profession," he explained, "but as an officer of the army, it is my duty and interest to be prepared for any situation that fortune or luck may offer. It is for this alone that I prepare and not for professional practice." Legal studies were not the only way Cump determined to improve his abilities as an officer. The study of geography also filled many idle hours, as he sought to gain a better understanding of how geographical and topographical features effected military tactics and strategy. He lamented the lack of a good atlas, however, and wrote home requesting that "you would procure for me the best geography and atlas (not school) extant." In this early stage of his career, Sherman had already grasped the importance of a successful military leader to be informed and well versed on a broad range of topics. Politics was not one of the topics that Cump devoted much time to. His family was heavily involved in politics, and Sherman considered himself to be a Whig, by virtue of the close affiliation his family had with that party, but he tried his best to stay clear of political issues and debates. Cump felt that it was an officer's "intention and duty to abstain from any active part in political matters and discussions, and for that reason I never permit myself to become interested in the success of either party." Still, he could not keep from speaking out when actions of the government went astride his basic morals and values. In referring to the forced relocation of the Creek, Chickasaw, Choctaw, Seminole, and Cherokee tribes of the southeast, to Oklahoma Territory, otherwise known as the trail of tears, Sherman showed a strong opposition to what he saw as an infamous act. "If a curse could ever fall upon a people or nation for pure and unalloyed villainy towards a part of God's creatures we deserve it for not protecting the Cherokees that lately lived and hunted in peace and plenty through the hills and valleys of northwestern Georgia."

In the winter of 1844–1845, Cump went on a deer hunting expedition in the Carolinas. He had an accident during this trip and sustained a serious injury to his arm, pulling it out of the socket. He was granted a medical leave, which he used to go home to Lancaster to mend. By the time he returned to Charleston, the eyes of the nation were fixed on the annexation of Texas into the Union and the possible war with Mexico that such a move might bring. The army prepared for the outbreak of hostilities, but Cump was not to be part of the buildup that was taking place. Instead of marching off to fight against General Santa Anna and his Mexican army, Sherman was destined to remain on garrison duty at Fort Moultrie. In 1844, he had written that "war as such is to be deprecated, but if it is necessary for the interests or honor of the country of course I may with perfect propriety rejoice at the opportunity of being able to practice what in peace we can only profess." Like most young officers, Sherman saw the coming clouds of war as a chance for distinction and promotion.

In the spring of 1846, Sherman finally got orders to leave Charleston, but he was not going to a theater of active operations. Instead, he was headed in the opposite direction. Detached from garrison service, in May, he was assigned to recruiting duty in Pittsburgh, Pennsylvania. Cump must have despaired to be given such duty when a war was about to be fought in Texas and Mexico, but his spirits must have risen when he received word that he was to relocate his recruiting efforts to

Zanesville, Ohio, a little more than 30 miles from Lancaster. Recruiting duty might not have been his choice of assignments, but his close proximity to home made it possible to spend time with family and friends. When word of the fighting between General Zachary Taylor's army and the Mexican forces at Palo Alto and Resaca de la Palma came, Cump determined to return to Pittsburgh to see if there were orders for him to report for active duty. "That I should be on recruiting service when my comrades are actually fighting is intolerable," he wrote. Upon reaching the city, he received a letter from Lt. Edward O. C. Ord telling him that his regiment was being sent to California, and urging him to make every effort to accompany it. Cump wrote to the Adjutant General, in Washington, asking to be relieved from recruiting duty and returned to active service, but he was too impatient to await a reply. Instead, he left a corporal in charge of his recruiting station and traveled to Cincinnati as fast as he could. When he reached the city, Cump reported to the commander of the military post in the city and asked to be given orders sending him to the front. When the colonel learned what Sherman had done, back in Pittsburgh, he sternly rebuked him for his dereliction of duty and commanded him to return to Pittsburgh immediately and resume command of his recruiting office.

Cump obeyed the order, but he did not do so as rapidly as the colonel had demanded. Instead, he stopped off at Lancaster for another visit with his family. When he eventually arrived at Pittsburgh, in June, he found that orders had been cut relieving him from recruiting duty and assigning him to Company F, Third U.S. Artillery, which was preparing to go to California. With no time to lose, Cump gathered together the items he would need and in a few hours was making his way to New York City, where the company was ordered to board ship to take them on the long journey through the Atlantic Ocean, around Cape Horn, and up the Pacific Ocean to California. Sherman had long sought assignment to a regiment serving in the far west, and now he was about to embark for duty in the westernmost point on the continent. His major concern at the present was reaching New York before his company sailed without him.

Sherman took a boat from Pittsburgh to Brownsville, where he boarded a stage for Cumberland, Maryland. From there, he traveled by train to Baltimore and Philadelphia, before making his final connection for New York. Arriving prior to the company's departure, Cump reported for duty to Captain Christopher Q. Thompkins, his company commander. First Lt. Edward O. C. Ord would serve as the company's senior first lieutenant, and Sherman would serve as junior first lieutenant. The company would be composed of 113 enlisted men and five officers, with many of the men in the ranks being new recruits. The *U.S.S. Lexington* was being prepared at the Brooklyn Navy Yard to transport the troops to California, along with the necessary supplies and provisions to subsist the men during their long voyage and after their arrival at their final destination. Because of the difficulty in supplying troops so far removed from military supply lines, the war department made the provision for the troops to draw six months' pay, in advance, so they could purchase commodities they would need during their expedition. Cump spent a large amount of this advance on extra clothing and other necessities he felt might be hard to find in California.

By July 14, 1846, all was in readiness, and the troops boarded the *Lexington* to begin their adventure to the Pacific coast. The ship was guided out of the harbor by a steam tug, and was soon plying its way across the waters of the open Atlantic. The sailing time from New York to Rio de Janeiro, Brazil, would take about 60 days, and "We soon settled down to the humdrum of a long voyage, reading some, not much; playing games, but never gambling; and chiefly engaged in eating our meals regularly. In crossing the equator we had the usual visit of Neptune and his wife, who, with a large razor and a bucket of soapsuds, came over the sides and shaved some of the greenhorns; but naval etiquette exempted the officers, and Neptune was not permitted to come aft of the mizzen-mast."

The *Lexington* arrived at Rio de Janeiro two months into its voyage, giving the ship's crew and soldiers a much-needed opportunity for shore leave. A week's time was allotted to reprovision the ship, and Cump took full advantage of this time to take in all the amenities offered by this famous port city. Visits to local merchants and artisans revealed treasures and oddities most of these Americans had never seen before. Sherman took in an opera at the local opera house, where he met the emperor of Brazil and his wife. He and several other officers dined at a famous French restaurant in the city, feasting on local fruits and delicacies "we had never seen before, or even knew the names of." At the end of the dinner, the waiter brought a check for 26,000 reis, which greatly alarmed Cump and his party. None of the Americans knew the rate of exchange between the U.S. dollar and the local currency, and it was feared that they did not have enough money to pay their bill. As it turned out, 1,000 reis was the comparable unit of measure to an American dollar, but it only had about half the value. In the end, the total for the meal was "about sixteen dollars." Sherman spent a great deal of time taking in the flora and fauna of the region, taking many hikes into the countryside. Cump was quite taken with Rio de Janeiro and thought it was one of the most beautiful places he had ever seen. At the end of the week, however, all hands were once more aboard the ship, and the next leg of the journey was undertaken.

In October, the *Lexington* arrived off the coast of Cape Horn and prepared to round the cape and sail into the Pacific Ocean. But a violent storm hit the area, buffeting the ship and causing a delay of nearly a month. Finally, favorable winds prevailed, and the *Lexington* made its way for Valparaiso, Chile, which was reached two months after leaving Rio de Janeiro. Sherman was far less impressed by this city and thought it to be on the shabby side. But it was November, or early spring, in that region, and he did avail himself of some of the local produce that was coming into season, including fresh strawberries. After replenishing the larder of the ship, the *Lexington* sailed out of Valparaiso's harbor for the final leg of the journey.

The ship was making for Monterrey, California, and, about the middle of January, it finally arrived off the California coast. The navigator overshot the entrance to Monterrey Bay, however, directing the ship to a point north of the harbor entrance. By the time the error was discovered and the ship turned around, a violent storm swept into the area, forcing the *Lexington* to remain at sea and ride out the waves for several days. When the storm subsided, the captain made his way for the harbor entrance and a secure port. The arduous journey was ended. It had taken 198 days from the time he had left New York City, but Sherman was finally in California.

Chapter 4

SERVICE IN CALIFORNIA

Cump liked what he saw of Monterrey. It was not the breathtaking city that Rio de Janeiro had been, but Sherman thought that "nothing could be more peaceful in its looks than Monterrey in January, 1847." The tranquil appearance of Monterrey belied events that had been taking place recently in California. The natives of San Diego were in open insurrection, and the U.S. fleet had sailed there to put down the uprising. General Steven W. Kearny, with a force of 300 men, had advanced from New Mexico to help in the pacification of California. On December 6, 1846, Kearny's command, along with a small force of Marines and volunteer militia, met a force of Mexican Lancers, under the command of Andres Pico. Kearny had the Mexicans outnumbered by more than two-to-one, and determined to attack immediately. The only problem was that most of his command was mounted on worn-out mules and their gunpowder had gotten wet and unserviceable. Kearny's mules and swords proved no match for Pico's well-trained horses and lancers, and the Americans suffered a humiliating defeat, with Kearny being wounded in the engagement. At Yerba Buena, a detachment of sailors performing forage duty had recently been assaulted. Col. John C. Fremont was on the scene with his California Battalion, approximately 400 strong, but the whole country was filled with guerillas. The men in Company F heard the news of recent events and imagined they would be called upon to defend themselves immediately upon landing at Monterrey. "Swords were brought out, guns oiled and made ready, and everything was in a bustle when the old *Lexington* dropped her anchor on January 26, 1847, in Monterrey Bay."

There was little cause for alarm, however, as all was quiet in Monterrey and its environs. In fact, all that remained of the war in California were some isolated pockets of guerillas. On January 13, 1847, the Mexican Californio forces were surrendered to Colonel Fremont when Andres Pico signed the Treaty of Cahuenga. The company disembarked from the *Lexington* and set up residence near a blockhouse, located on a hill overlooking the town. Soon after leaving the ship, a small village of tents popped up on the hillside, as supplies were unloaded from the *Lexington* and stored in a nearby warehouse. Cump had been assigned the duties of quartermaster officer and commissary officer for the company, so he took a room in the custom house and did not live in the tent city with the rest of the men. In his role as quartermaster, he would be responsible for acquiring and distributing necessary items such as clothing, shoes, tents, and all other such articles needed to maintain a company in the field. As commissary officer, he was responsible for obtaining food to feed the troops. In New York, he had been entrusted with $8,000 for the quartermaster needs of the company, and $20,000 for the commissary. Cump found that his commissary duties would be fairly easy to fulfill. There were numerous cattle in Monterrey, and these could be purchased for $8.50 each, so the men would have an ample supply of beef. This could readily be augmented by the vast variety of game animals found to be in abundance around Monterrey, including elk, deer, geese, and ducks. Produce, of all varieties, were both plentiful and inexpensive. Sherman's only real problem concerning commissary issues were items like coffee and sugar, both of which were extremely scarce and expensive. Regarding his quartermaster duties, Cump had purchased a large quantity of clothing before leaving New York. In fact, he had bought enough shirts that he felt the company would not need to worry about that article for three years.

Affairs in California were not nearly as bleak as Cump and his comrades had been led to believe when they first arrived at Monterrey. True, there were not many American troops in California when they had disembarked from the *Lexington*, but substantial reinforcements were on their way. Col. Jonathan D. Stevenson commanded a regiment of New Yorkers that would arrive in March. Col. Philip St. George Cooke was leading a battalion of Mormons from Utah and would reach California that same month, as would Col. Richard B. Mason, the grandson of founding father George Mason, and the officer the war department had selected to eventually succeed Kearny as military governor of California. In addition, the U.S. Navy had more ships arriving off the coast of California, including the battleships *Ohio* and *Columbus*. The *Columbus* had been patrolling waters off the coast of China and was under the command of Commodore James Biddle. Upon his arrival, Commodore Biddle assumed command of all naval forces in the region.

Sherman and his comrades had seen no action, and there had been more infighting between American commanders than any other confrontations since Company F had landed at Monterrey. Col. Fremont set himself up in Los Angeles as military governor and had been disputing General Kearny's authority. Fremont had accepted the surrender of the Mexican forces in California and felt that justified his claim to become military governor. All other military commanders in California acknowledged Kearny's seniority and right to command. Fremont, a noted frontier explorer, felt that he was entitled to overall control in California by virtue of the expeditions he had led through the region, thereby making him better acquainted with the residents and the surroundings. Kearny tried to get rid of Fremont by removing him and his volunteers from the army. He sent Colonel Mason to Los Angeles with orders to muster Fremont and his volunteers into the U.S. service, pay them, and immediately thereafter muster them out of the service. Fremont refused to allow the mustering of his men to take place, however, and a violent argument took place between him and Mason, resulting in a challenge for a duel between the two men. Although the affair of honor never took place, Kearny and Fremont were no closer to resolving the rift between them. Nonetheless, Fremont had become worried by the proceedings, and he determined to travel to Monterrey to meet with General Kearny. Upon meeting with the general, Kearny delivered a menacing rebuke to his wayward subordinate, ordering him to return to Los Angeles to disband his volunteers, and warning him against any further efforts to exercise control in the area. Fremont had established his camp about a mile outside of town, and Cump took the opportunity to pay a visit to the famous frontier explorer. Sherman spent about an hour visiting with Fremont, but related that he was "not much impressed with him."

Among the reinforcements that had arrived in California was Captain William G. Marcy, who assumed the duties of commissary officer for the troops at Monterrey. Col. Thomas Swords took over the quartermaster duties for the garrison, leaving Sherman with no extra responsibility above being a company officer. Cump was forced to vacate his accommodations in the custom house and take up residence in one of the company tents. But Sherman did not have to stay in his tent for very long. General Kearny took him for detached duty as a staff officer for an important mission to Los Angeles. Fremont had returned to the city, but he failed to follow Kearny's directive to disband his forces. Kearny planned to go to Los Angeles himself, to settle the matter once and for all, and Sherman was to accompany him.

When the pair arrived in Los Angeles, Kearny directed Cump to go to where Fremont was living to instruct Fremont that he wished to see him. Fremont accompanied Sherman back to the place where Kearny had set up residence, and the two officers closeted themselves together. In the end, Kearny not only prevailed, he brought Fremont up on court martial charges, which led to Fremont's resignation from the army. Cump spent several days in Los Angeles and was very impressed with the abundance of vineyards in the region. While in the town, General Kearny made preparations for his return to the East, and for turning over the military governorship of California to Col. Richard Mason. Captain Tompkins, Cump's company commander, planned to go with Kearny, leaving Lieutenant Ord in command of the company, and Sherman as second-in-command. Colonel Mason had other plans for the young lieutenant, and he assigned Sherman to be his adjutant general.

Mason was an army veteran of 30 years, having received his commission in 1817. He had served in the Black Hawk War, before being assigned as major of the First U.S. Dragoons. He had a reputation as being a strict disciplinarian and having a stern and rigid demeanor. Mason took a liking to Sherman, and displayed none of those traits in front of his new adjutant. Cump found him to be kind and agreeable, and felt he had "a large fund of good sense." Sherman enjoyed listening to Mason's stories about such notable military commanders as Winfield Scott, David Twiggs, William Harney, Zachary Taylor, and William Worth, and he felt that his superior exhibited unlimited confidence in his abilities.

The war was still being fought in Mexico, but all was quiet in California, and Cump would have no opportunity to distinguish himself on the field of battle. There were some small actions taking place in what was called Lower California, or the Baja Peninsula, but they were of a limited scale, and under the direction of the navy. For Sherman, service in California would consist of paperwork and administrative duties. His shooting was confined to hunting, and Cump evidently did a great deal of that. In his memoirs, he talks about hunting much of the local game, expressing particular delight over his hunts for ducks and geese. It seems that these water fowl were so numerous, at certain times of the year, Sherman said he could "load a pack mule" with ducks and geese in the amount of hunting that could be done in one evening and the following morning.

The year 1847 passed lazily by in Monterrey. Lieutenant Ord, and the rest of Company F, occupied their time building a fort, in which they mounted several pieces of cannon taken from the *Lexington*. Colonel Mason's days were filled with many executive decisions concerning the civil administration of California, and Sherman passed his time in the adjutant general's office, his staff consisting of one clerk and a civilian interpreter. On February 2, 1848, the war with Mexico officially came to a close with the signing of the Treaty of Guadalupe Hidalgo. The U.S. Army, in Mexico, became an army of occupation, not an army of conquest. For Cump and his comrades, the conclusion of the war meant that there would be no opportunity to gain military distinction on the battlefield. There were the usual rounds of balls and parties to entertain the soldiers and pass away idle hours, but there was nothing really exciting about duty in California. That changed in the spring of 1848, when two men came into Cump's office, seeking Colonel Mason. Sherman escorted them to the office of the military governor, which adjoined his own, and went back to his own desk. Shortly thereafter, Colonel Mason came to his door and called for Cump to join them.

Several pieces of paper lay on the colonel's table, opened to expose their contents. Mason told Sherman to take a look, and after a short examination, Cump asked, "Is it gold?" Sherman suggested the samples be tested. He first took one of the nuggets and bit it with his teeth, proclaiming it to be indeed metallic in nature. Next, taking a hatchet, he beat the largest sample flat. The metallic nature, the malleability, the weight; all seemed to confirm the fact that this was indeed gold.

The gold had come from Sutter's Mill, along the American Fork of the Sacramento River. John Sutter was building a sawmill at the site, and the gold was found by John Marshall, the foreman of the construction crew Sutter had hired to build the mill. Sutter and Marshall had already tested nuggets found by Marshall before alerting Colonel Mason of the discovery, and had come to the conclusion that it was gold. For his part, Sutter was unhappy about the discovery, as he knew that word of a gold strike would bring a flood of treasure hunters to the region and would ruin his plans to make the area an agricultural center for California. Sutter's fears would soon be realized. When word of the strike was made public fortune-seekers descended on California in droves. It is estimated that more than 300,000 people, from the United States, and all around the world, came to the state during the gold rush, which started in 1849. San Francisco had been a sleepy little town of some 200 inhabitants in 1848. A couple years later, it was a thriving city, boasting a population of more than 26,000.

In late June 1848, Cump made a personal expedition to Sutter's Mill. Since the time that the first sample came into Colonel Mason's office, there had been a constant stream of rumors coming from Sutter's Mill. Reports of men taking $500 to $1000 a day filtered back to Monterrey, and gold fever took hold of those people already living in California. Soldiers began to desert from the army to strike it rich in the gold fields, and prices for goods began to rise at an alarming rate. Sherman persuaded Colonel Mason that they should go to Sutter's Mill, in person, and see for themselves what was taking place there, so that they could more accurately report the situation to the government. After an arduous journey, they arrived at the gold fields. Mining camps were found all up and down the river from Sutter's Mill, and all was hustle and bustle along the river's banks, as prospectors worked to extract the gold from the river's bed. Cump and Mason spent a week sizing up the situation before returning to Monterrey, where Sherman drafted a letter to the adjutant general of the army relating the magnitude of the gold discovery. There was no mail service to California, so it was decided that the letter would be carried to Washington by a lieutenant who had recently been promoted, and thereby was entitled to a furlough.

As fortune-seekers poured into California, the question of civil authority in the region was brought to the forefront. California had been ceded to the United States by the Treaty of Guadalupe Hidalgo, signed by the Mexican government on February 2, 1848, thus making it a U.S. territory. From the time Colonel Mason assumed the responsibilities of military governor, he had left most of the details of local government in the hands of native Californians. Mason felt that California's status as a U.S. territory meant that Congress should take the lead in setting up the civil government. He felt uneasy about administering military rule in what was no longer conquered territory, but a part of the United States. The swell of emigrants agreed with Mason. The majority of newcomers railed at military control, demanding civil authority in California. Congress, however, was divided over California's status, owing to an ongoing argument over the expansion of slavery. The question would not be answered until the Compromise of 1850 allowed California to enter the Union as a free state. In the meantime, Colonel Mason grew weary of the political situation and resigned his post as military governor in November 1848. He was replaced by Brig. Gen. Persifor F. Smith, in February 1849, at which time he returned to his home in Missouri. He died, at Jefferson Barracks, on July 25, 1850, at the age of 53.

General Smith's arrival brought with it a promotion, of sorts, for Sherman. He was replaced as adjutant general for the Department of California, and was assigned to Smith's staff, in that same capacity, for the Division of the Pacific. Colonel Mason had performed his duty in California in as wise and honorable a fashion as anyone could have expected of him, but the conditions General Smith found, on his arrival, would have tested the resolve of a lesser man. The gold frenzy that had taken hold of the region created numerous problems for the military. General Smith determined to retain headquarters for the Department of California in Monterrey and to establish headquarters for his Division of the Pacific in San Francisco. This proved a futile undertaking.

Gold fever had demoralized the city, and profiteering was the order of the day. Men could not be hired for less than an ounce of gold per day, and a room in one of the shabby hotels cost $1,000 per month. All but one of the servants Smith and his staff had brought with them deserted for the gold fields, and General Smith and his family were reduced to poverty, being able to secure only one descent meal a day on his army salary. Everything was in a state of chaos, and mob rule was in effect. The harbor in San Francisco was littered by some 600 ships, a ghost fleet that had been abandoned when the crews deserted their vessels to search for gold. The situation became so critical that supply ships arriving at the city would turn over their crews, as prisoners, to a U.S. Navy vessel until the cargo was unloaded. The captain would then claim his crew again for the return voyage home. General Smith could not hope to maintain his headquarters in San Francisco, so after a short stay in the city, he returned to Monterrey, where preparations for a permanent relocation to Sonoma could be made.

There was little military duty to perform in California, so General Smith both allowed and encouraged his officers to enter into any business ventures they could to augment their army pay. Sherman secured employment as a surveyor to lay out a proposed town at the mouth of the San Joaquin River, named the New York of the Pacific. For his services, Cump was paid $500, and given several lots of land within the limits of the town. Though the New York of the Pacific failed to materialize, and proved to be a failed venture for its speculator, Cump was able to sell several of his lots and realized another windfall of $500. The $1,000 he made from his surveying allowed Sherman to better maintain himself amid the skyrocketing inflation in California.

In January 1850, Cump applied for an extended furlough to go home and visit his family. A leave of six months was granted by the war department to allow Sherman to visit the family he had not seen in a few years. Cump first went to Ohio, to visit his mother, before making his way to Washington. The Ewing family had relocated to the nation's capital, as Thomas Ewing's political activities forced him to spend an increasing amount of time there. As one of the nation's leading members of the Whig Party, Ewing's power and influence had increased during the time Cump was in California. In 1849, he had become the country's first Secretary of the Interior, and the following year, he was appointed to fill the vacancy created when Thomas Corwin resigned from the U.S. Senate. This would be Ewing's second term in the Senate. As a past Secretary of the Treasury and Secretary of the Interior, and close friend of both Daniel Webster and Henry Clay, he wielded considerable political clout and was a force to be reckoned with in Washington. His duties in the city had become so taxing, and his time so short, that he moved the family from Ohio to a stately house on Pennsylvania Avenue, near the White House, in order to be able to spend time with them.

Cump's arrival in Washington must have been the fulfillment of a dream for both him and Ellen. In all the years that had transpired since he had reported as a cadet at West Point, in 1836, there had been precious little time for the two to be together. Two furloughs from the academy, one from South Carolina, and the visits while on recruiting duty in Zanesville had been the sum total of the time spent with each other in 14 years. But separation had not weakened the bond between them, and the affection and attraction they felt for one another was as strong as it had been when Sherman had first left Ohio to begin his military career. They shared their lives in letters throughout those years, though Cump's time in California must have been a particular hardship, with the infrequent and painfully slow delivery of mail to the Pacific Coast. Ellen Ewing was now a 26-year-old woman, an old maid by the standards of the day. Cump was 30, himself, and well past the age when most of his contemporaries had settled down and taken a wife.

Neither Cump nor Ellen seemed to be worried about the passing of time, however, as both had been convinced of the eventual consummation of their love. That moment came during Sherman's furlough from California. A wedding date was set for May 1, 1850, and preparations were made for one of the grandest events on Washington's social calendar that year. The wedding ceremony was held at the Ewing mansion, on Pennsylvania Avenue, and the guest list included a who's who of Washington's elite and powerful. President Zachary Taylor was there along with his entire Cabinet. Also in attendance were such notable political giants as Senators Daniel Webster, Henry Clay, and Thomas Benton. Cump and Ellen were the center of attention, and once the ceremony was concluded, they received the congratulations and well wishes of the most powerful and influential people in the nation. When Henry Clay's turn came to congratulate the happy couple and kiss the bride, he presented Ellen with a bouquet of flowers. Following an elaborate and lively reception, the newlyweds took their leave of the gathering to begin their honeymoon to Baltimore, Niagara Falls, and Ohio. The first of the couple's eight children, Maria Ewing Sherman, would be born nine months later, on January 18, 1851. Over the coming years the union would bear seven more children: Mary Elizabeth would be born on March 17, 1852; William Tecumseh Jr., on June 8, 1854; Thomas Ewing on October 12, 1856; Eleanor Mary on September 5, 1859; Rachael Ewing on July 5, 1861; Charles Celestine on June 11, 1864; and Philemon Tecumseh on January 9, 1867. All of the Sherman children would be raised in the Catholic faith, and Thomas would eventually become a priest. Two of the children would die during the Civil War: William Tecumseh Jr., in 1863, at the age of nine, and Charles Celestine, in 1864, in infancy.

After a honeymoon lasting two months, the couple returned to Washington in July. They had been in the city for only a few days before President Taylor suddenly died. Cump attended Taylor's funeral as an aide-de-camp, at the request of the adjutant general of the army, though he was still only a first lieutenant. Thomas Ewing's resignation as Secretary of the Interior and his appointment to the U.S. Senate took place during this time, and Cump assisted the family in moving out of the house on Pennsylvania Avenue and back to Lancaster, Ohio. That September, Sherman rejoined his regiment, now at Jefferson Barracks, in St. Louis, Missouri. Ellen followed him, and the couple set up residence in a private dwelling in the city on Chouteau Avenue. That same month, the commissary department of the army was increased, allowing four additional captains, and Cump was appointed to one of the vacancies. His commission as captain was dated September 27, 1850. It had taken him more than 10 years of service, but Sherman had finally been elevated above the rank of lieutenant.

Chapter 5

CIVILIAN PURSUITS

Post life at Jefferson Barracks, and in St. Louis, was a prolonged honeymoon for Cump and Ellen. The barracks were still the largest military installation in the United States and boasted one of the most active social calendars in the country. The birth of the couple's first child in January 1851 made Cump officially a family man, and started him thinking about the added responsibility of providing for a family and the need to find a vocation outside the military. A captain's pay did not allow for many comforts or luxuries, and there was little hope that Sherman would soon receive promotion to a higher rank. The 10 years he had waited to be raised to captain was commonplace in the old army, and he was not sure he could wait another 10 years to receive another raise in pay.

The Sherman's second child, Mary Elizabeth, was born on March 17, 1852. By this time, Cump was seriously considering the prospect of leaving the army. That summer, Ellen and the children went back to Lancaster, to live with her parents, while Cump remained in St. Louis. That September, he was ordered to report for duty in New Orleans. Ellen and the children joined him there, but in February 1853, they departed for Ohio. The thought of another lengthy separation from Ellen was more than Cump was willing to bear, though he dutifully accepted the assignment. Early in 1853 he applied for a six-month furlough to go home and visit his family. By the end of this leave, Sherman had made up his mind to resign his commission and seek his fortune in civilian pursuits. On September 6, 1853, Cump tendered his resignation from the army. For the last 17 years, all his adult life, he had been in the uniform of a U.S. officer. Now, he would venture into the private sector. After careful deliberation, Cump decided that he could best make a living by entering into the profession of banking. With all the growth and investments in California, and armed with his knowledge of the region and the contacts he had made while serving there, he settled on making a new life for himself and his family on the West Coast.

Sherman became a partner in Lucas, Turner & Co., which planned to open a bank in San Francisco. Major H. S. Turner had been a friend of Cump from the army who had gone into partnership with James Lucas, a prominent financier in St. Louis and the principal owner of the Lucas & Symmonds bank in that city. Lucas and Turner planned to open a branch office of the bank in San Francisco, and offered Sherman a junior partnership in the venture. Turner was to go to San Francisco to establish the bank, but, having family and home in St. Louis, he did not want to stay there for an extended period. He suggested to Lucas that Cump would be a fine addition to the partnership, and a perfect person to take over for him once the bank was up and running. Sherman said that Lucas offered "me a very tempting income, with an interest that would accumulate and grow." Lucas wanted Sherman to relocate to San Francisco, permanently, and assume the responsibilities of being the head of the firm in California. Cump would be paid a substantial salary, far exceeding the amount he was making as a captain in the army, and would also receive interest in the firm, without the necessity of investing any of his own money. Being the head of a respected firm would also bring a level of prestige for him and his family. It was the sort of offer Sherman had been hoping for, and the timing seemed right.

In February 1853, with his family bound for Ohio Sherman began his long journey to California to evaluate the situation and make his final decision as to whether he would accept the offer made by Lucas. This time, he would not be making the exhaustive trip around the tip of South America, however. Instead, he booked passage on a steamer bound for Nicaragua. From there, he cut across the country on the Nicaragua River and lake to the Pacific Ocean, where he secured passage to California aboard the *S.S. Lewis*. The trip was definitely shorter in duration than the one he made when first detailed to California during the Mexican American War, but it turned out to be one of the most perilous journeys he had ever taken. The *Lewis* was off the coast of California, not far from San Francisco, when the ship hit a reef. "About 4 a.m. I was awakened by a bump and sort of grating of the vessel, which I thought was our arrival at the wharf in San Francisco," Sherman recalled, "but instantly the ship struck heavily; the engines stopped, and the running to and fro on the deck showed that something was wrong." Sherman leapt from his stateroom and was shortly standing on the deck of the *Lewis*. The ship had already sunk, but being in shallow waters, the deck was still above the level of the ocean. The passengers were soon shuttled to shore in boats, and Sherman struck out down the beach to find out exactly where they were. He soon came to Bantinas Creek, where he found a schooner waiting for the tide to rise so it could sail over the bar and out into the ocean. The schooner was bound for San Francisco, and Sherman obtained permission from its captain to go along as a passenger. He wrote a note to the captain of the *Lewis*, telling him where they were, and explaining that he had gotten passage to San Francisco and would send help for them directly. But this was not to be. The schooner had been to sea for only a few hours when it ran into a squall that threw the ship over on its side. Many of the crew and passengers, including Sherman, were catapulted into the water. All aboard survived the accident, and were picked up by a passing ship on its way to San Francisco, and so Cump arrived in the city, delayed, water-loggers, and somewhat the worse for wear, but still very much alive. He immediately alerted the authorities as to the plight of the crew and passengers of the *Lewis*, and a ship was dispatched to rescue them.

After satisfying his questions about the firm and finding suitable lodging for himself and his family, Cump finally accepted Lucas's offer and submitted his resignation to the army. He then set sail for New York, arriving in the city in July of 1853. From New York, he made his way to Lancaster, where he and his family prepared for a move to the

Pacific coast. By September, all was in readiness, and the family sailed from New York, reaching San Francisco on October 15. The family took lodging in a hotel, and Sherman devoted his full attention to learning everything he could about the banking business, with Turner serving as his mentor. His time of instruction was short-lived, however, as Turner left for New York in November, turning responsibility for the firm over to Sherman. Although still a novice in financial affairs, Cump soon realized that the expenses of the bank meant that the firm was operating at a slight loss. Lucas felt that earnings could still be achieved because the bank was obtaining gold in California for a lower price than its market value in New York, but this proved to be incorrect. Sherman had been right in his estimation of the bank's earning potential, or lack thereof. He could depend on his salary, but there would be no additional income derived from profits to the firm.

The bank operated at a slight loss throughout 1854, but in 1855, it was faced with a serious crisis that threatened to bankrupt the firm. During that year, Henry Meiggs, a local businessman and entrepreneur, caused a financial collapse in San Francisco that ruined several banking establishments. Meiggs secured loans, all over the city, accumulating over $1,000,000 in debt. When he fled town with his family for Chile, it caused a run on the banks of the city, and several establishments could not meet their financial obligations and were forced to close their doors. Lucas, Turner & Co. had also loaned money to Meiggs, but the amount was not substantial. Most bankers in San Francisco trusted Meiggs completely, but Cump felt there was something shady about the man. He insisted on Meiggs reducing his debt to the firm at a time when other bankers were offering him an almost unlimited line of credit, and he secured much of that debt with liens on Meiggs's property. Lucas, Turner & Co. suffered a loss when Meiggs fled town, but because of Sherman's foresight, it was limited to only $10,000.

The financial crisis of 1855 spilled over into the following year. 1856 witnessed a decline in property values, as the economy of California became depressed. Numerous businesses failed, and worried investors began withdrawing their capital from San Francisco. Lucas, Turner & Co. was still solvent, and enjoyed a prominent reputation in the city, but Cump realized the futility of the continued operation of the bank. He advised Lucas of his belief that the firm should be dissolved, and the senior partner agreed. The bank continued to operate until April 1857 and closed its doors only after notifying all of its depositors and allowing them to withdraw their savings. Sherman's banking venture had ended in failure, but it had been conducted in an honorable fashion from beginning to end.

Cump's reputation as a banker and businessman in San Francisco, along with his previous military service, led to his commission as a major general in the California Militia in 1856. In May of that year, San Francisco witnessed a struggle between opposing political factions in the city that erupted into violence. Democratic Mayor James Van Ness was accused of political corruption by William T. Coleman, and when one of his supporters was killed in a duel for speaking out against the administration, Coleman took action by calling his followers to form a Vigilante Committee. The vigilantes armed themselves and entered into open hostilities with city authorities, even storming the jail to remove the man who had fought in the duel and another prisoner who had shot a U.S. Marshall the previous year. Both men were hung by the vigilantes on May 20, 1856. Mayor Van Ness appealed to Governor John Neely Johnson to call out the militia to restore order in the city, and Johnson ordered Sherman to procure all available arms and muster the California Militia in San Francisco on June 2. Cump tried to comply, but soon discovered that there were almost no weapons with which to arm the volunteers. Johnson ordered Brig. Gen. John E. Wool to issue muskets to the militia from the army arsenal at Benicia, but Wool refused to comply. Wool stated that Johnson did not have the authority to demand arms or men from the army, as they were in federal service, and could only be ordered into action by the president. Sherman and Johnson were furious over Wool's decision. There was nothing they could do to overturn it, however. Cump resigned his commission in the state militia and vowed never again to take part in California politics.

Cump's short-lived tenure as a major general in California, followed, as it was, by the failure of the bank, left no reason for him or his family to remain in California. On May 1, 1857, the Sherman's bid farewell to California, and set out for New York City. Mr. Lucas was opening a branch of his bank there and had retained Sherman to oversee its operation. Major Turner was also involved in the venture, and the branch would have the same name of Lucas, Turner & Co. that had been used in California. By July 21, Cump and Turner had rented an office, hired a staff of three people, and officially opened the branch. Sherman's initial efforts in New York were fruitful, and it appeared that this financial venture would bear profits for the firm that had been anticipated in California. Cump was doing business with some of the largest and most respected financial institutions in the city. Sherman had reason for optimism that he had finally found his civilian calling. But that optimism was to be short-lived, as the economic crisis that had crippled California followed Cump to the East Coast. By the end of August, the financial decline on the West Coast caused Eastern bankers to become wary of loans to western investors. The decline in land values in the west slowed migration, and caused the value of railroad stocks to plummet. Many Eastern banks had invested heavily in the railroads and were faced with large losses. When a number of railroads failed, it sent a shock wave across the financial institutions of the nation, but the breaking point came when one New York bank, the Ohio Life Insurance & Trust Company, failed due to faulty railroad investments. The sinking of the S.S. *Central America*, bound from California with a cargo of $1,600,000 in gold only added to the financial gloom. The resulting panic caused by these events led to a nationwide depression.

Lucas, Turner & Co. were caught up in this financial panic just as the firm had been in San Francisco. The conduct of Sherman and the bank under his direction was also the same as it had been in California. No investor in Lucas, Turner & Co. lost any of their funds because of the financial panic. Although the New York branch was forced to close due to the economic conditions, Sherman and his partners demonstrated the highest degree of responsible management of their affairs, and earned the respect of the entire financial community. On January 30, 1858, Sherman published a notice announcing the dissolution of the firm. Although he would make yet another trip to California in an attempt to settle the accounts of the firm, Cump was now officially out of the banking business. His first attempt at civilian pursuits had ended in failure, despite his competent administration of the firm's affairs. By July 1858, Cump was back with his family in Lancaster. "I was perfectly unhampered," he wrote in referring to his lack of employment, "But the serious and greater question remained, what was I to do to support my family, consisting of a wife and four children, all accustomed to more than the average comforts of life?"

Cump considered his options and talked with Thomas Ewing about what he could do. Ewing had interest in coal and salt mines in Ohio and offered Sherman a position managing them. Cump wished to be as independent as possible, however. Desiring to make his own way in the world, and not be taken care of by his adopted father, he turned the offer down. Instead, he chose to go into a partnership with two of Ewing's sons, who were dealing in land speculation in Leavenworth, Kansas. On January 1, 1859, the firm of Sherman, Ewing & McCook was formed, and Cump became the senior partner in the land development corporation. Business was good, but profits were not large enough to sustain all of the partners and their families. Accordingly, Sherman removed himself from the firm and began farming on a tract of land some 40 miles from Leavenworth. The agricultural venture held little promise of substantial financial gain, so Sherman was still left with no means of supporting his family.

By June 1859, Sherman considered his plight to be desperate, and decided that he would not be able to make a living in the private sector. Despairing of success, he once fitfully proclaimed that he was "doomed to be a vagabond." Civilian ventures lacked the order and discipline that had been the basis for so much of his adult life. Accordingly, he wrote a letter to Major Don Carlos Buell, the assistant adjutant general, inquiring if there were any positions open in the army to which he could be reinstated. Cump was especially interested in a position in the paymaster's department, but was willing to accept any posting available. Buell responded that there were no vacancies for Sherman in the army, but he did have a suggestion that would allow Cump to make use of his army experience. The state of Louisiana was forming a military college and was seeking a suitable candidate to become superintendant of the institution. Sherman sent a hurried letter of introduction to Governor R.C. Wickliffe, expressing his desire to be considered for the position, and detailing his military training and experience. Cump's application was turned over to the board of supervisors, for consideration, and in July 1859 he received a letter from Governor Wickliffe informing him of his selection as superintendant, and requesting him to come to Louisiana at his earliest possible convenience. Cump's salary as superintendant was set at $5,000 per year.

The Louisiana State Seminary of Learning & Military Academy, as the institution was to be named, was the first college-level institution of higher learning to be established in the state. Located just outside Alexandria, it would later become the Louisiana State University. It had found its origin in several land grants made by the U.S. government for the purpose of establishing an institution of higher learning and was a forerunner of the land grant universities chartered by the federal government in 1862. Cump traveled to Baton Rouge in the fall of 1859 to meet with Governor Wickliffe and make preparations for the first class of cadets at the seminary. Wickliffe provided Sherman with an introduction to Governor-Elect Thomas O. Moore, who would be taking office in January 1860, and would succeed him as president of the board of supervisors for the school. Moore lived in the same parish as the seminary, as did Gen. George M. Graham, chairman of the board, so Sherman departed Baton Rouge to meet with the supervisors of the school and to inspect the facilities.

Moore pledged his entire support to the school, and in Graham, Cump found an enthusiastic and energetic patron whose whole purpose was to make the school a success. Graham and Sherman worked out all the details of the school during their visit, before taking a ride out to visit the property. The faculty had already been established by the board of supervisors, and would consist of Sherman as superintendant and professor of engineering; Francis W. Smith was commandant of cadets and professor of chemistry; Anthony Vallas the professor of mathematics and philosophy; David F. Boyd the professor of English and ancient languages; and E. Berti St. Ange the professor of French and modern languages. It was a small staff, to be sure, but was considered sufficient to handle the needs of the school at the time.

The school itself was quite another matter. It consisted of a large, attractive house, situated on 400 acres of ground. While the structure was spacious enough to accommodate both housing the cadets, as well as classrooms, it was completely devoid of furnishings. Cump found a carpenter living at the house, serving as a sort of caretaker for the property. He noticed that there was a large pile of lumber stacked in front of the building and set about obtaining the items he would need to open the school. Hiring four more carpenters to assist the caretaker, Sherman put them to work turning the pile of lumber into tables, chairs, beds, blackboards, and anything else he could think of that would be needed. He took a room in the seminary for his lodging, so as to be able to closely supervise the activities. By early November, progress was such that a decision to open the school on January 1, 1860, was reached. Accordingly, on November 17, 1860, Governor Wickliffe issued a proclamation announcing the opening of the seminary and seeking applicants. According to the terms of the charter, 16 members of the first class were to be admitted on scholarship, with no charge for their tuition. These would be required to pay for only their books and clothing. The rest of the applicants would pay $343 per year for their tuition. The classroom and military instruction was to be modeled after West Point, but this first class would be without uniforms or muskets. Late in 1859, Cump made a trip to New Orleans to purchase mattresses, books, and other necessary items, and by the end of the year all was in readiness to welcome the incoming class.

On January 1, 1860, 60 cadets reported to the inaugural class. Several more cadets were added during the winter, bringing the total number to 73. All proceeded in accordance with the plans laid out by Sherman and General Graham, and the instruction went forward unimpeded. Sherman noted several deficiencies in the charter for the seminary, and he took the opportunity, during this first session to bring them to the attention of the state legislature. Working with the legislative committee formed to oversee the seminary, he helped draft a new bill that placed the school on better footing. A prominent feature in the bill allotted one scholarship appointment from each of the 56 parishes in the state. The legislature readily passed the bill and allotted the lofty sum of $35,000 a year for the maintenance of the school. As a Northerner, Sherman had been viewed by some in Louisiana as an outsider. His brother, John Sherman, was serving in the House of Representatives, and was seeking the post of Speaker of the House. John was viewed by many as being an abolitionist who sought to interfere with the political and economic institutions of the South, and this made them suspicious of Cump. Sherman's complete devotion to his duties at the seminary, combined with his strict avoidance of political issues, won him the complete confidence of all he came in contact with, however, and earned him the esteem and respect of many of the most prominent men in the state.

The first year of instruction ended with examinations held on June 30 and 31, 1860, followed by an elaborate ball. With classes ended, all students and faculty were free to go home and visit their families for the summer, and November 1 was set as the date that instruction would be resumed. Cump went home to Lancaster, to visit his family, but this was not to be a vacation for the superintendant. After only a few days, he set out for Washington, to meet with John B. Floyd, the secretary of war, in an effort to procure muskets for his corps of cadets. Louisiana had already received its allotment of arms from the federal government, but Floyd readily agreed to provide 200 cadet muskets, along with all necessary equipment, and promised to have them shipped to the seminary before classes commenced in November. From Washington, Cump next traveled to New York, where he met Francis Smith. There, the two men purchased uniforms, textbooks for beginning a school library and arranged for their shipment to Louisiana. With his business concluded, Cump returned to Lancaster and his family. A more permanent reunion was already in the works. Two frame structures were being built on the campus to house the families of the married professors at the seminary, Professor Vallas and himself; the work was proceeding nicely. Cump hoped that they would be completed soon, so he could relocate Ellen and the children to Louisiana.

When Cump returned to the school he found the local citizens in an aroused state, caused by the impending presidential election, due to take place on November 6. Abraham Lincoln was not even on the ballot in Louisiana, or in eight other states of the Deep South. Locals doubted that this Illinois upstart could actually capture the White House, but Lincoln's strong support in the Midwest and North worried them. If the Republicans did win the election, without one vote from any of the Deep South states, it would serve as proof that Southern interests were no longer represented in the federal government and would probably signal the breakup of the Union. Most of the citizens Cump came in contact vowed the state would secede if Lincoln were elected. For his part, Sherman kept clear of any political arguments and went about his duties at the school, welcoming back his returning cadets and his second class of undergraduates on November 1. All told, there were now approximately 130 students attending the seminary, and Sherman had them divided "into two companies, issued arms and clothing, and began a regular system of drills and instruction, as well as the regular recitations." The house that was to serve as a dwelling for Cump and his family had been completed, but he moved into it alone. To Ellen he wrote that he would wait to send for her and the family until the classes were fully commenced, but, in reality, the delay was due to "the storm that was lowering heavy on the political horizon."

Cump's premonition proved to be correct. On November 6, 1860, Abraham Lincoln was elected to the presidency, despite the fact that he had not won a state south of the Mason–Dixon Line, and had not received a single vote in nine of the Deep South states. The South saw the election of Lincoln as evidence that Southern rights were no longer represented in the national government, and steps were taken to back up their threats of secession as soon as word of Lincoln's victory was made known. South Carolina was the first to take action, passing an ordnance of secession on December 24, 1860. From January 9 to 11, 1861, Mississippi, Florida, and Alabama all ratified ordnances of secession and left the Union, followed by Georgia on January 19 and Louisiana on January 26. By February 1, 1861, all the states of the Deep South had left the Union, and a convention was called in Montgomery, Alabama, where Jefferson Davis would be named president of the newly formed Confederate States of America.

On January 18, Sherman was sure that the secession convention called in Louisiana would be successful in taking the state out of the Union, and he wrote a letter to Governor Moore about his feelings on the matter. "Sir: As I occupy a quasi-military position under this State, I deem it proper to acquaint you that I accepted such position when Louisiana was a State in the Union, and when the motto of the seminary was inserted in marble over the main door: 'By the liberality of the General Government of the United States—the Union, Esto perpetua.' Recent events foreshadow a great change, and it becomes all men to choose. If Louisiana withdraws from the Federal Union, I prefer to maintain my allegiance to the old Constitution as long as a fragment of it survives, and my longer stay here would be wrong in every sense of the word. In that event I beg you will send or appoint some authorized agent to take charge of the arms and munitions of war here belonging to the State, or direct me what disposition should be made of them. And furthermore, as president of the board of supervisors I beg you to take immediate steps to relieve me as superintendent the moment the State determines to secede, for on no earthly account will I do any act or think any thought hostile to or in defiance of the old Government of the United States. With great respect, etc., W.T. Sherman."

Governor Moore responded on January 23, expressing his deepest regrets over Cump's decision to leave the seminary, but pledging him "the respect, confidence, and admiration, of all who have been associated with you." He directed Sherman to transfer all school property to Professor Francis Smith in the eventuality that the state's secession made Cump's resignation necessary. Dr. S. A. Smith, a member of the board of supervisors, wrote to Sherman in an attempt to change his mind about resigning his post. Smith told Sherman that he would "say nothing of general politics, except to give my opinion that there is not to be any war." He went on to express his admiration for Cump by inquiring if it were not "possible for you to become a citizen of our State?" Sherman was true to his word, however, and when Louisiana voted to secede from the Union he prepared to turn over all property and accounts to Francis Smith and vacate his position as superintendent. This was accomplished by February 19, 1861, when he officially resigned and took his leave from the school. While formally bidding farewell to his cadets, Sherman placed his hand over his heart and told them they were all "right here." Most of these young men would soon be joining the Confederate army, and Cump might well face them on a future field of battle, but for now, they were merely youths whom Sherman held in high esteem.

It was with deep regret from all parties concerned that Sherman took his leave from the seminary. Cump had loved the school and poured himself fully into making it a first-rate establishment of higher learning. Those connected with the institution came to regard Sherman as an intelligent and highly capable administrator, and it was with sad hearts that they bid farewell to their superintendent. On April 1, 1861, the Academic Board of the seminary sent Cump a letter stating "That in the resignation of the late superintendent, Colonel W.T. Sherman, the Academic Board deem it not improper to express their deep conviction of the loss the institution has sustained in being thus deprived of an able head. They cannot fail to appreciate the manliness of character which has always marked the actions of Colonel Sherman. While he is personally endeared to many of them, as a friend, they consider it their high pleasure to tender to him in this resolution their regret on his separation, and their sincere wish for his future welfare." The actions of the board were faithful to their words. Sherman's portrait, as the first superintendent, continued to hang in the school throughout the four bloody years of the Civil War. At a time when many in the South hated and cursed his name, Sherman remained a respected and honored patron of higher learning in this section of Louisiana.

Chapter 6

THE OUTBREAK OF THE WAR

Sherman chose his course of action based on his conviction that his allegiance was due to the federal Union and to the oath he had taken to protect the government and the Constitution upon graduating from West Point. The issue of slavery does not seem to have played a part in his decision one way or another. Over the years, he had spoken out against the manner in which slaves were used or treated. He had even advocated that they be taught to read and write, and had stated that illiterate slaves were worth less than those who had been educated. Indeed, Cump liked Southerners, enjoyed their company and lifestyle, and seemed to have no reservations about the institution of slavery, as a whole. The peculiar institution played no role in his decision to resign his position as superintendent and make his way north.

In casting about in search of employment, Cump contacted H. S. Turner, his partner from banking days. Turner had secured a position as superintendent of a street railroad in St. Louis for Sherman at the salary of $2,500 per year. Sherman left New Orleans on March 1 and made his way for Lancaster. Before leaving for St. Louis, he made a trip to Washington to see his brother. John Sherman had just been appointed to the Senate to fill the unexpired portion of Salmon Chase's term, following Chase's appointment to President Lincoln's Cabinet. Cump was interested in finding out if there was any need for his services with the army, given all the talk of impending war that was being bandied about. John took Cump to meet Lincoln and introduced him to the president as Colonel Sherman, just lately arrived from Louisiana. Lincoln asked Cump his impression of affairs there at the time of his departure and received the answer that the people of Louisiana were preparing for war. Lincoln dismissed Sherman's warning by flippantly stating "Oh, well! I guess we'll manage to keep house," and with that Cump's interview was ended. Sherman was so enraged by Lincoln's nonchalant manner that he entered into a tirade pointed at his brother in which he condemned all the politicians he blamed for placing the country in this precarious situation, stating that these same politicians could fix the mess they had created with no help from him. He would go to St. Louis with his family and have nothing further to do with the government or its war.

St. Louis offered no escape from the war, however. The residents were in a high state of agitation, brought on by anticipation of armed confrontation between the U.S. forces and the large pro-Southern elements within the city. Missouri's governor, Claiborne F. Jackson, was a staunch supporter of the Southern cause, and it was feared that his intention was to take the state out of the Union to join the Confederacy. The federal arsenal in St. Louis was of particular concern, as the weapons and ammunition it contained could be used to facilitate Jackson's agenda if they fell into Southern hands. Captain Nathaniel Lyon arrived in St. Louis in March 1861, and through his friendship with Francis P. Blair Jr., he was appointed commander of the arsenal. Lyon became involved with a group called the Wide Awakes, a paramilitary organization, made up largely of German pro-Union men from the city. The Wide Awakes were secretly provided weapons from the armory in an effort to counter what Lyon saw as a growing threat from Governor Jackson and his supporters. When President Lincoln made his call for troops to put down the Southern rebellion, Missouri was given a quota of four regiments. Governor Jackson refused to provide the men. Instead, he called out the Missouri State Guard and ordered the troops to gather outside St. Louis, at Camp Jackson, for the alleged purpose of training.

The Missouri State Guard was approximately 700 strong when it gathered at Camp Jackson and was commanded by Brig. Gen. Daniel M. Frost. Although the militia had committed no subversive acts against the federal government and continued to fly the U.S. flag over its encampment, Lyon felt its presence a threat to the arsenal and the city of St. Louis, so long as it was under the command of Governor Jackson. A personal reconnaissance of the camp confirmed Lyon's fears when he noted that the militia possessed cannon taken from the arsenal. On May 10, Lyon decided to make a pre-emptive strike and erase the threat. 5,000 Union troops were assembled and marched out to Camp Jackson. General Frost's forces were surrounded, and Captain Lyon demanded their immediate surrender. Vastly outnumbered, and caught in the open, Frost had no choice but to comply with Lyon's demand. When Lyon's men marched the prisoners back to the city, they were greeted by throngs of angry pro-Southern citizens who lined the streets. Tensions grew as impassioned citizens gave expression to the outrage they felt over this perceived unlawful act. Passion erupted into violence when shots rang out from the crowd and several of Lyon's men were struck. The soldiers returned fire, and the scene instantly became one of horror and confusion. Some 29 citizens were killed and as many as 60 were wounded. Lyon was able to reach the safety of the arsenal with his soldiers and their prisoners, but the incident touched off several days of rioting and violence in the city that eventually led to the establishment of martial law.

Cump and his family had arrived in St. Louis just in time to be caught up in these dramatic events. When Captain Lyon marched his column out of the city, Cump had refused the invitation of some friends to tag along with the soldiers and watch the fun, explaining that "in case of conflict the by-standers were more likely to be killed than the men engaged." Instead, he paced up and down the street in front of his house, listening for any sounds that would indicate the commencement of a battle. His son, Willie, then seven years old, accompanied him. No fighting was to be heard, however, and, at length, the head of Lyon's column was seen marching into the town. As Cump described it, "I again turned in the direction of Camp Jackson, my boy Willie with me still. At the head of Olive Street, abreast of Lindell's Grove, I found Frank Blair's regiment in the street, with ranks opened, and the Camp

Jackson prisoners inside. A crowd of people were gathered around, calling to the prisoners by name, some hurrahing for Jeff Davis, and others encouraging the troops. Men, women, and children, were in the crowd. I passed along till I found myself inside the grove, where I met Charles Ewing and John Hunter, and we stood looking at the troops on the road, bending toward the city." The situation was growing more tense by the second, but for some reason the column was halted right where it was, in the middle of the road. Sherman saw Major Rufus Saxton, commanding the battalion of regular army troops in the column, and he approached Saxton to give him an evening newspaper. At this point, a drunken fellow from the crowd tried to make his way through the troops to the people gathered on the opposite side of the street. "One of the regular file-closers ordered him back, but he attempted to pass through the ranks, when the sergeant barred his progress with his musket 'a-port'. The drunken man seized his musket, when the sergeant threw him off with violence, and he rolled over and over down the bank." By the time the drunken man picked himself up and made his way back to the street, the regulars had marched on, and a regiment of Home Guard, under the command of Colonel Peter J. Osterhaus was passing by. The drunken man held a pistol in his left hand as he approached Osterhaus's column, which he fired at close range, striking one of Osterhaus's officers in the leg. The soldiers of the Home Guard responded by firing over the heads of the crowd, hoping to disperse the mob before any more violence took place. Cump and his son were caught in the middle of the confused scene. "Charles Ewing threw Willie on the ground and covered him with his body. Hunter ran behind the hill, and I also threw myself on the ground. The fire ran back from the head of the regiment toward the rear, and as I saw the men reloading their pieces, I jerked Willie up, ran back with him to a gallery which covered us, lay there until I saw that the fire had ceased, and that the column was moving on, when I took Willie and started for home round by way of Market Street." Sherman was not in the army, but he had been under fire for the first time in the Civil War.

On May 14, Cump received a message from his brother informing him that he had been appointed to command the 13th U.S. Infantry, with a rank of colonel, and imploring him to come to Washington at once to accept the command. Sherman met with Ewing and Hunter to

seek their counsel, and both men advised him to accept the commission. He hastily made his preparations to depart for Washington, leaving Ellen and the children in St. Louis. Cump thought that he would
soon return to the city to recruit volunteers to fill out his regiment,
so he felt no apprehension over leaving his family. Upon arriving in
Washington and reporting to Lt. Gen. Winfield Scott, he discovered
that he would be forced to remain in the capital. At once, he sent word
to Ellen to pack up their belongings and move the family back to the
Ewing home in Lancaster.

The 13th U.S. Infantry was a new regiment and existed only on
paper at the time Sherman reported to Washington. Cump had expected to recruit and train the volunteers for the regiment when he
arrived at the capital, but an order from General Scott assigned him to
Scott's staff in the capacity of an inspector general. As such, it would
be his responsibility to inspect the volunteer regiments that were pouring into the city from all over the North. President Lincoln had called
for 75,000 volunteers to put down the rebellion, but Sherman felt that
number was utterly inadequate. Having spent considerable time in the
South, and being quite familiar with Southern sentiments and resolve,
Cump was convinced that the Lincoln administration was underesti-
mating the capacity and determination of the Southern people.

During this time, there were two Union armies operating in the
Eastern Theater: Brig. Gen. Irvin McDowell's forces, in and around
Washington, and Brig. Gen. Robert Patterson's army, located in the
vicinity of Williamsport and Hagerstown, Maryland. These forces were
situated so as to confront the two Confederate armies in the theater
of operations. Brig. Gen. Pierre G. T. Beauregard commanded a Confederate army facing Washington, in the vicinity of Centreville and
Manassas, Virginia. Brig. Gen. Joseph E. Johnston led a second Southern army, located at the head of the Shenandoah Valley, and opposed
to Patterson's force. Cump's brother, John, was serving as a volunteer
aide of Patterson's staff, and Sherman determined to pay him a visit.
He caught up with Patterson's column on the march to Williamsport
on July 1–2. Cump took the opportunity to renew acquaintances with
George H. Thomas, his old roommate from West Point, who was leading a brigade in Patterson's army. Several other officers in Patterson's
command were well known to Sherman, and he had an enjoyable

reunion with these comrades from his past. The focus of their discussions centered around the war. Most of the officers were convinced that the war would be short in duration, that a simple show of force would be all that was necessary to induce the Southerners to sue for peace under the old flag. Cump was not so easily convinced. Before the opposing armies ever met on the field of battle, he envisioned a long and bloody conflict that would take years and cost untold numbers of lives before the nation could be reunited. But his opinion was definitely in the minority among the eager and enthusiastic officer of Patterson's command. Most felt the war would be little more than a lark, a fleeting chance for glory and adventure, and many agreed with a politician's statement that all the blood spilled in the fighting could be wiped up in a single handkerchief.

John Sherman was due to take his seat in the Senate, as Congress had been called into session on July 4, so he resigned his position as a volunteer aide and returned to Washington. Cump accompanied him back to the capital and was encouraged to learn of the administration's efforts when Congress convened. President Lincoln had asked Congress to authorize the raising of 400,000 additional troops to defend the Union and recapture federal property that had been lost to the Confederates. This latest assessment of the government was more in line with Sherman's own thoughts. Cump was sure that the Confederates could not be threatened or coerced into abandoning their newly formed government and renewing their old allegiance with the national government. He knew that a vast army would be needed to conquer Southern territory and bring the seceded states back into the Union by force.

Gen. Winfield Scott cautioned the administration to move slowly in the persecution of the war. His advice was to wait to mount a general offensive until the Union volunteers had the opportunity to be properly drilled in military tactics and had been transformed from an armed mob into an army of trained soldiers. The press and the public had taken up the cry of "On to Richmond!," however, and the Lincoln administration was feeling the pressure. The public clamor for action caused Lincoln and Simon Cameron, his secretary of war, to disregard Scott's advice and order an advance on Richmond to begin the middle of July. General McDowell was given his marching orders and obediently prepared the army to take the offensive. Of prime importance was the command structure of the army. Scott took steps to place the right officers in critical positions of responsibility, and Sherman was to benefit from the restructuring. When Scott promoted Col. David Hunter to take command of the Second Division of the army, Sherman was selected to assume command of Hunter's old brigade. When the army moved forward, Cump would be at the head of the Third Brigade in the First Division, under the command of Brig. Gen. David Tyler. Sherman's brigade consisted of the 13th New York, 29th New York, 69th New York, 79th New York, and Second Wisconsin infantry regiments, and Captain Romeyn B. Ayres's battery of the Third U.S. Artillery.

Sherman was delighted with his command believing it to be among the finest brigades in the army. He soon found himself embroiled in what threatened to be a mutiny in the 69th New York. This regiment, made up of Irish immigrants from New York City, had enlisted for 90 days service in early April. They left New York for Washington shortly after their enlistment, but had been delayed in reaching the capital for over a month, due to being re-routed by way of Annapolis instead of going through Baltimore because of the riots that had taken place in the latter city when the Seventh New York had marched through earlier in the month. When July rolled around, the men of the regiment asserted that they had served their 90 days and demanded to go home. The problem was that the enlistment papers they had signed stated that their 90-day service did not begin until they were officially mustered in to the federal service, which did not take place until after they reached Washington. According to their enlistment papers, their term of service was not expired until the beginning of August, and the government intended to hold them to their agreement. Col. Michael Corcoran, commander of the regiment, wanted to take part in the expected upcoming battle, as did most of his officers, but many of the men in the ranks felt that they had done their duty and were demanding to be allowed to go home. The whole matter was turned over to the war department, which rendered a decision that the men would be held to the letter of the enlistment papers they had signed. Their service had not officially begun until they were mustered in to federal service, and the 90 days would be calculated from that date.

Sherman found another of his regiments to be in need of attention. The Second Wisconsin was commanded by Col. S. Park Coon, recently a doctor of that state, and a man possessed with little or no military training or knowledge. His second in command was Lt. Col. Henry W. Peck, a West Point graduate and a trained officer. Cump did not want to take this regiment into battle with a novice in command and preferred to have Peck leading it. He settled the matter by having Colonel Coon transferred to his personal staff, which made Lieutenant Colonel Peck commander of the regiment.

On July 15, the army marched out of Washington in the direction of Richmond. Sherman's brigade had been reduced to four regiments in the campaign. The 29th New York had been left behind as part of the force detached from the main army to occupy the city's fortifications and guard the capital. In all, General McDowell would be leading an army of some 35,000 men, the largest such force ever to be gathered on the North American Continent. He had named it the Army of Northeastern Virginia. Near Manassas Junction, General Beauregard waited for McDowell with approximately 22,000 men, in what he had named the Army of the Potomac. In less than a year the names of the armies would be virtually switched. The Union army would become the Army of the Potomac and the Confederate army would be called the Army of Northern Virginia, and both of those forces would cover themselves with glory and everlasting fame.

Cump missed out on the fighting in the Mexican American War and had spent the entire duration of the conflict on outpost duty in California. It seemed certain that things would be different in this war, however. He was marching into the fray at the head of a brigade and was almost assured of being in the thick of the action. As the army filed out of its camps around Washington and started to march south, Cump must have thought that he was finally going to be able to put his many years of military training and experience to good service on the battlefield. The prospect of finally seeing action did not cause him to be swept away in the moment, though. The army might be going forward to engage the foe, but Cump was not overly optimistic. "I still regard this as but the beginning of a long war," he confided.

Chapter 7

BULL RUN

Regiment after regiment marched out of Washington to the sound of martial airs played by their bands. Julia Ward Howe watched with patriotic excitement as the bands and throngs of men gaily went forward to what most of them thought would be a great adventure. Julia listened as one of the bands played an old revival tune that caught her fancy. She would later add words to the melody, and the resulting song "The Battle Hymn of the Republic" would become the anthem of the Northern armies. The march of the Union army toward Manassas was a slow and tedious process, however. The men in the ranks were not accustomed to moving in large formations, having not yet mastered the intricate maneuvers of army drill. The heat was stifling, and the dust raised from the unpaved road by horses, wagons, and tens of thousands of marching feet filled the air with a choking cloud that made it hard for the men to breathe. Thousands of footsore and exhausted men fell out of the ranks to lay prostrate along the sides of the road. Wild blackberry bushes were to be found along the line of march, and many other soldiers bolted from their places in the ranks to pick the refreshing berries. Cump was dismayed by the actions of the soldiers. He said that "The march demonstrated little to save the general laxity of discipline;

for with all my personal efforts I could not prevent the men from strag-gling for water, blackberries, or any thing on the way they fancied." At the end of two days of marching, Colonel David Hunter's Second Divi-sion arrived at Fairfax Courthouse, Virginia, little more than 20 miles from Washington.

The slow pace of the Union army foiled McDowell's plans thus far. He intended to take the Confederate garrison at Fairfax by surprise, but the defenders had ample time to make good their escape. Col. Samuel P. Heintzelman's Third Division had skirted the town, and marched toward Bull Run, in an effort to develop the Confederate right flank. General Tyler's division, of which Sherman's brigade was a part, was behind Hunter's in the line of march, and upon reaching Fairfax Court-house, Tyler was ordered to march on through the town, toward Centreville, and the fords of Bull Run Creek beyond. McDowell desired Tyler to make a demonstration against the Confederate position to oc-cupy their attention. In this way, he hoped to be able to mask Heintzel-man's flanking movement from observation. Tyler was ordered to make a noisy and convincing demonstration, but McDowell was quite clear in cautioning him, "Do not bring on an engagement." Tyler moved his division forward with Col. Israel B. Richardson's brigade in the lead. Upon reaching Centreville, the bulk of Tyler's division stopped. Tyler, along with Richardson's brigade, pushed on toward Blackburn's Ford on Bull Run Creek.

Tyler was flushed with victory and was caught up in the chase. Cen-treville had been captured without a fight. The Confederates retreated from the town, toward Bull Run, and Tyler reasoned they would con-tinue to run if pressed with a vigorous pursuit. Two miles south of Cen-treville, Tyler found an elevation from which he could clearly see Bull Run, Blackburn's Ford, Mitchell's Ford, and Manassas, some three miles beyond. McDowell had ordered that only a demonstration be made, but Tyler now entertained the possibility of crossing Bull Run and cap-turing Manassas. He ordered Richardson to bring up his command and positioned two 20-pound pieces of artillery and had them open fire to develop the enemy position. Two companies of the First Massachusetts Infantry were sent forward as skirmishers. The skirmishers had hardly begun before they drew the fire of Confederate marksmen concealed in houses and trees on the north side of the stream. Confederate resistance increased as the Massachusetts men neared the stream, and when they had almost reached their objective, they were caught in a deadly cross fire from concealed Southern units on either flank. The skirmishers were forced to retreat, just as the bulk of Richardson's brigade arrived on the scene. One of McDowell's staff officers was with Richardson's main body, and upon examining the situation, advised Tyler against making any further efforts to force his way across the stream. Caught up in the excitement of the moment, Tyler declined his advice. Richardson was ordered to advance, and four regiments were formed to make the attack. What Tyler did not know was that half of General Beauregard's entire army was directly in front of him. As his regiments formed in line of battle, enemy fire from their front increased to the point that Tyler was convinced to call off the charge. Orders did not reach Richardson until after he had already sent the 12th New York Infantry forward, however. The New Yorkers marched straight into a murderous volley that caused the survivors to throw themselves to the ground. This regiment was facing Brig. Gen. James Longstreet's entire 2,500-man brigade, along with reinforcements from Brig. Gen. Jubal Early's brigade. The men of the 12th New York endured the fury of the Southern fire for half an hour before breaking for the rear in a rout. Longstreet then ordered two of his regiments across the stream to attack the First Massachusetts Infantry. Colonel Richardson wanted to rally the New Yorkers and send his entire brigade forward in a counterattack, but Tyler had seen enough. He ordered Richardson to disengage and pull his men back. General McDowell arrived on the scene just as Richardson's men were withdrawing from their exposed position. He gave Tyler a severe rebuke for exceeding his orders. The fighting at Blackburn's Ford was ended, save for an artillery duel that lasted a couple hours.

Sherman and his brigade had been a couple miles in the rear of Richardson's command when it made contact with the Confederates. "From our camp, at Centreville, we heard the cannonading, and then a sharp musketry fire. I received orders from General Tyler to send forward Ayre's battery, and very shortly after another order came for me to advance with my whole brigade. We marched the three miles at the double-quick, arrived in time to relieve Richardson's brigade, which was just drawing back from the ford." This was the first time Cump's men had been under fire, and the scene they marched through was one of confusion. Wild-eyed men, fleeing from the field were the first to greet them, followed by wounded who were frantically trying to reach a place of safety. Sherman encouraged his men and tried to set a manly example to keep the terrible sights and sounds from unnerving them. The brigade was formed in line of battle, and though they were not sent forward, several men were killed by Confederate artillery fire. Tyler ordered his entire division back to Centreville, and the action for the day was ended. The mission had gone far beyond McDowell's intentions, but Tyler had definitely developed the enemy position. Beauregard's army was on the other side of Bull Run Creek, and the Confederates had no intention retreating further.

McDowell and Beauregard kept their armies in camp from July 19 to 20, while each general planned their strategy. An urgent call had gone out to Joseph E. Johnston, in the Shenandoah Valley, to come to Manassas with all possible haste. Robert Patterson had been charged with using his army to prevent such a move, but Johnston was able to give the cautious Patterson the slip and march to Beauregard's aid. For the first time in the history of warfare, trains were used to transport Johnston's troops part of the way to Manassas. Johnston arrived, with the vanguard of his army, on the afternoon of July 20. Being senior in rank, Johnston should have assumed command of both armies when he arrived on the field, but his lack of knowledge about the ground on which the battle was to be fought caused him to defer and leave Beauregard in charge.

McDowell and Beauregard both intended to attack in the upcoming battle. In fact, both men adopted exactly the same strategy, choosing to hold on their left flank and attack with their right flank. If the attacks were launched simultaneously, it would have the effect of both armies spinning around a central axis like a top. Beauregard wrote out his orders to his subordinate commanders with lavish Napoleonic flair, and many of his directives were too complicated for his inexperienced subordinates to comprehend. Indeed, some of his orders were so complex as to cause Beauregard himself confusion. In one instance, if the orders had been strictly obeyed, Beauregard had actually ordered one Confederate unit to attack another. The Confederate commanders did not have to worry about carrying out these complex plans, however, because McDowell launched his attack before Beauregard. The Southerners would be fighting on the defensive.

During the night of July 20, preparations were made to attack the Confederates at dawn of the following day. At 2:00 A.M., the troops were roused from their beds and the assaulting columns were marched forward. Hunter's and Heintzelman's divisions were to march to the right, to Sudley's Ford, where they were to cross Bull Run and attack the enemy left flank. Tyler was to march straight ahead, to the middle fords of the creek, and keep the enemy occupied until the flanking movement was completed. He was then to cross the creek and attack. Col. Dixon Miles's small division of just two brigades was held in reserve. McDowell's plan began to unravel from the start. Tyler was ordered to move out first, causing Heintzelman and Hunter to be delayed. Since Tyler had the least distance to travel, his division should have been the last to march forward, and Heintzelman and Hunter should have been allowed to get in position before Tyler's demonstration began. McDowell realized the error an hour into the march and ordered Tyler to get his men off the road and allow the other divisions to pass. But valuable time was being lost as confused troops stumbled and groped their way through the inky darkness.

Brig. Gen. Robert Schenck's brigade was the first of Tyler's division to reach their objective at the Stone Bridge. They did not arrive until 5:00 A.M., however, and the signal shots from a 30-pounder cannon to announce to the rest of the army that they were in position were not fired until an hour later. Sherman's brigade followed Schenck's, and he arrived on the field shortly thereafter. Cump deployed his brigade into line of battle and waited for further orders. But these orders were not forthcoming. Schenck's division waited for about four hours for the flanking divisions of Hunter and Heintzelman to get into position. Finally, at about 10:00 A.M., Cump observed an enemy regiment in his front pulling out of its place in line and marching quickly toward Sudley's Ford. It was obvious that the Confederates had discovered the movement being made upon their flank and were taking steps to counter it. When Sherman saw another massing of enemy troops intended to reinforce their left flank, he ordered his artillery to open fire. Captain Ayres had but two of his four cannon with him, however. Both of his rifled pieces had been detached, and his remaining smooth-bore guns proved inadequate to reach the massed enemy columns. Sherman sent word to Tyler, requesting the return of rifled cannon that had been detached, and listened while the sounds of fighting across the creek to his right signified that Hunter and Heintzelman had become engaged. The roar of battle grew closer, and Cump could tell that the Confederates were retiring before the Union assault. At noon, the sounds of the battle became static, and it was soon clear that the Southerners were making a stand. General Tyler was ordered to advance his division across the stream and attack the Confederate positions in his front, in support of the flanking movement.

Cump ordered his brigade forward, using a ford in the stream that a Confederate officer had unwittingly made known to him. The rebel had ridden out into Bull Run to shout insults to the Federals on the opposite bank, and, in so doing, exposed this shallow crossing to Cump's watchful eyes. "We found no difficulty in crossing over," Sherman wrote, "And met with no opposition in ascending the steep bluff opposite with our infantry, but it was impassible to the artillery, and I sent back word to Captain Ayres to follow if possible."

Sherman found little resistance. Only Brig. Gen. Nathan Evans's troops, a small brigade consisting of two regiments, a squadron of cavalry, and two artillery pieces, barred the crossing at Bull Run. This opposition was further diminished when Evans discerned McDowell's intentions and surmised that Tyler's division was merely a diversion to the real assault. Picketts brought word of the Federal column approaching Sudley's Ford, confirming Evans's suspicions. Realizing that "it was not the intention of the enemy to attack me in my present position," Evans shifted troops to his threatened left flank, and these were the troop movements Sherman observed. Leaving only four companies from the Fourth South Carolina Infantry to confront Tyler, Evans marched the remainder of his command to oppose Hunter and Heintzelman. Instead of preparing a line of defense against the overwhelming odds against him, Evans attacked the Union horde head on. The Union vanguard was made up of two Rhode Island regiments, under the command of Col. Ambrose E. Burnside, of Hunter's division. Hunter was riding with these regiments when Evans's Confederates opened fire. The Rhode Island troops were staggered and stopped by the first volley. Hunter attempted to rally the troops, but fell seriously wounded in the neck and left cheek. Burnside hurriedly brought forward the rest of his brigade. Although the Confederates were greatly outnumbered, the fierceness with which they fought convinced Burnside that the opposite was true. In fact, Burnside felt that he was at a disadvantage, and that he was facing a minimum of six enemy regiments and two batteries of artillery. The Confederates added to Burnside's misconception when Col. Roberdeau Wheat led 500 men from his First Louisiana Battalion, known as Wheat's Tigers, forward to attack the Federal position. Wheat's action seemed foolhardy. He was assaulting an entire Union brigade with about half a regiment, and the vast disparity in numbers should have resulted in the complete annihilation of his entire command. Events turned out to the contrary, though. The attack caught the Federals off guard, and threw their lines into confusion. The Tigers would be repulsed, but their rash and impetuous attack bought time for Beauregard to send reinforcements to the threatened area.

Brig. Gen. Bernard Bee's brigade was the first to arrive, followed closely by that of Col. Francis Bartow. Bee formed a line on the right of Evans, and Bartow's brigade formed on Bee's right. Captain John Imboden, Bee's artillery commander, placed his cannon on Henry House Hill, and began to bombard the Federal line. Evans now felt more secure in his position, but the danger to the Confederates was increasing by the moment as more Union troops crossed Bull Run and formed into line of battle. Evans, Bee, and Bartow now had 5,500 men in position to resist the Federals, but they were still outnumbered by almost three-to-one, and a determined assault by the Federals would surely chase them from the field. The Confederate commanders decided not to wait, but to take matters into their own hands. In an attempt to emulate Wheat's prior success, all three Southern brigades surged forward to attack the Federals in their front at approximately 10:30 A.M. The assault met with withering fire from the Union infantry, and Union artillery tore gaping holes in the Confederate lines. Still, they pushed onward, until the hopelessness of the enterprise became apparent. General Bee's brigade advanced further than Evans's or Bartow's, and found itself not only taking fire from the front, but from both flanks, as well. All three brigades were forced to fall back, and as Bee's command crested the slope of Matthews Hill and hastened down its southern slope, they spied a gray-clad regiment approaching from the direction of the Stone Bridge, which was thought to be reinforcements.

These gray-clad troops were not Confederates, however. They were members of the Second Wisconsin of Sherman's brigade. Uniforms for the opposing sides were not yet standard, and the Wisconsin men were wearing gray militia uniforms adopted by the regiment before the outbreak of hostilities. The men of Bee's Fourth Alabama Infantry, thinking the Wisconsin troops to be friends, hailed the Federals and prepared to form in line of battle on their right flank. When the Alabama boys unfurled their colors, the Second Wisconsin let loose with a volley that decimated their ranks and left the Alabama regiment confused and reeling. It was soon apparent to Evans, Bee, and Bartow that they were facing Federal forces on their flank as well as to their front. Facing only token resistance from the four companies of the Fourth South Carolina, Cump pushed his brigade forward, toward the sound of the guns, with the Second Wisconsin in the lead. His action placed his command squarely on the flank of the Confederates and in a position to roll up their entire defensive line. The Alabama troops retreated under the fire poured into them by the Second Wisconsin. The Confederate line was crumbling and for the moment it seemed as if the day belonged to McDowell.

Beauregard was left confused and indecisive by these events. The left flank of his army had been severely battered and was in danger of being rolled up and forced from the field. Clearly, the danger to his army came from that sector and all of his efforts should have been focused toward providing these troops with all the aid he could muster. But Beauregard became caught up in the excitement and seemed unable to think clearly. He ordered brigades back and forth across the Bull Run as he vacillated between reinforcing his left and launching his own offensive against Centreville. Finally, General Johnston settled the matter by proclaiming the Confederate left was where the battle had been joined and where it must be fought out. From that point on, Beauregard concentrated all his efforts on relieving the pressure on his left flank and made no further plans to initiate an attack.

Following the withdrawal of the Fourth Alabama, Sherman met Burnside and Col. Andrew Porter on Matthews Hill. The three brigade commanders surveyed the situation and concluded to press their attacks onward. General McDowell, who was nearby, observed the scene and came to the same conclusion. The Confederates were in retreat all along their line, and it seemed that one more push would drive them from the field. A drive of three miles would place the Union army in possession of the Manassas Gap Railroad, spelling doom for Beauregard and his army. Anticipating the complete destruction of the rebel army, McDowell was seen riding along his lines, standing up in his stirrups and shouting encouragement to the men for a final victorious rush: "Victory! Victory! The day is ours!"

Victory should have gone to the Union that day. The three brigades of Evans, Bee, and Bartow had been driven from their position and were badly battered. The rest of Beauregard's army was confused and in no position to contest an immediate assault by the superior forces confronting them. The problem was that the assault was not made immediately. The brigades belonging to Burnside and Porter had been roughly handled by the Confederates and were themselves disorganized. Precious time was spent in bringing order to these brigades in preparation for the final assault, and that time was used to advantage by the Confederates. Col. Wade Hampton arrived on the scene with his 600-man South Carolina Hampton Legion. Upon reporting to General Bee, just prior to the collapse of the Confederate line, Hampton was instructed to take a defensive position on Henry House Hill and hold his troops in reserve. Hampton decided to disregard Bee's instructions and, forming his men into line of battle, he ordered them forward. Hampton's troops marched down the slope of Henry House Hill just as Bee's line broke and began its retreat to the rear. The terrified survivors of the Fourth Alabama passed through Hampton's ranks as the South Carolina troops pushed forward into the blazing fury of Union musket and artillery fire. Hampton's command took fearful casualties and soon discovered that all other Confederate units had fled from the field, leaving the South Carolina men to stand alone against the Federals. After several minutes spent facing a murderous fire, Hampton ordered his men to retreat to the cover of a wooded depression 700 yards northeast of the Henry House.

It seemed nothing could stop the Union advance. Every Confederate attempt to make a stand had been crushed, and McDowell's army stood on the threshold of complete victory. McDowell formed his line for the final push. Erasmus D. Keyes's brigade was placed on the left, Sherman's brigade occupied the Union center, and Porter's brigade was on the right, reinforced by the brigades of Orlando Wilcox and William B. Franklin. But the sacrifice made by Hampton's Legion had bought time for more Southern reinforcements to reach the field. Brig. Gen. Thomas J. Jackson's Virginia brigade, five regiments strong, had recently arrived and taken up a defensive line on the reverse slope of Henry House Hill. Jackson occupied a strong position, on high ground, and instead of ordering his men forward to the support of their be-leaguered comrades, he instructed them to lay down and conceal themselves from enemy fire. Only his artillery, under the command of Col. William N. Pendleton, was ordered into action, but the fire from these 13 guns could not stem the Union tide or reverse the fortunes of Evans, Bee, and Bartow. As the defeated Confederates swept back past Jackson's position, General Bee stopped to address Jackson. "General, they are beating us back!" he cried. Jackson calmly responded, "Sir, we'll give them the bayonet." Jackson's answer gave Bee new spirit, and he hurried back to rally his men for another stand. Pointing to Henry House Hill, he exclaimed there is Jackson, standing "like a stone wall," and exhorted his troops to reform behind the Virginians. Victory seemed a foregone conclusion for the Union army, and the Confeder-ates were giving ground all over the battlefield, but this was the high tide of Northern fortunes.

Jackson ordered his brigade to hold their position and prepare to repulse the Federal advance. The men of Col. Arthur C. Cummings's 33rd Virginia Infantry were not content to wait for the Yankees to come to them, however. Instead, the men of the regiment surged forward, without orders, to attack the enemy at the base of Henry House Hill. Uniforms had not yet become standardized, and the men of the 33rd Virginia were attired in blue. The approach of Cummings's men was seen as a hostile act by many of the waiting Federals, but the blue uni-forms served to confuse them. Believing the advancing troops to be a Union regiment, the Federals withheld their fire. Their mistake was not realized until the 33rd Virginia's line halted, raised their muskets, and let loose with a devastating volley. The fire killed and wounded many of the men and horses in the batteries of Captains Charles Griffith and James Ricketts, and demoralized the 11th New York Infantry, which had been supporting the batteries. Jackson, watching from the crest of the hill, ordered the rest of his brigade to charge, and for the first time the shrill Rebel Yell was heard on a battlefield. The survivors of the two Union batteries and the 11th New York retreated, and Jackson's men swarmed over the position, capturing the enemy cannon.

For the next two hours, the battle raged along the base of Henry House Hill. The guns of Griffith's and Ricketts's batteries changed hands several times, as neither side had the horses at hand to draw them from the field. Sherman's brigade was hotly engaged during this part of the battle. He had been ordered to commit his regiments to the fighting one at a time in piecemeal fashion. General McDowell still had superior numbers of troops on the field, but instead of throwing them forward in one resistless charge, he was sending them into the fight in parcels, and the management of Sherman's brigade was, in microcosm, a representation of how the entire engagement was being fought. The Second Wisconsin was the first to be sent forward. Still dressed in their gray militia uniforms, the men of the Second Wisconsin were fired upon not only by Confederates, but also by Union comrades who mistook them to be enemy troops. Badly cut up and demoralized, they were forced to retire. The 79th New York was Sherman's next regiment to join the fray. This regiment was led by Colonel James Cameron, brother of Secretary of War Simon Cameron. The 79th advanced toward the brow of Henry House Hill amid a storm of shot and shell from a Confederate battery, and a hail of withering musket fire. The charge faltered several times, but the men were rallied and the assault pushed forward. The fighting was severe, and casualties in the 79th New York continued to mount. The men of the regiment were finally fought out and retreated from the field. Among their fallen was Colonel Cameron, who had been struck down leading one of the numerous rallies.

Col. Michael Corcoran's 69th New York was the last of Sherman's regiments committed to the maelstrom. The 69th was made up of Irishmen, and in addition to the national colors, they marched behind a blazing green Irish banner. Colonel Corcoran led his men forward into the incessant fire of enemy cannon and small arms. By this point in time, Beauregard and Johnston had been able to gather sufficient reserves on this part of the field to outnumber the Union forces attacking them. The Irish advanced gallantly, but were facing an impossible task. For a short time, they held their ground, finally being compelled to retire by the murderous fire constantly thinning their ranks.

Sherman was present all over the field as his regiments fought. He could be seen galloping among the men, issuing orders and giving words of encouragement. A piece of canister had scratched his knee, a spent bullet had struck his collar, and his horse had been wounded in the leg. Being a soldier all his adult life, Cump had fortified himself against the reality of men falling in battle. This was his first battle, however, and he was not prepared for all of the horrible scenes now spread before him. The sight of men, dead and mangled in every perceivable manner, seemed to have little effect upon him, but the plight of innocent animals shook him to his very core. He reported seeing riderless horses, their eyes glazed by pain and fear, spouting blood from horrific wounds as they ran from the conflict, and artillery horses, "lying on the ground hitched to guns, gnawing their sides in death." The man who would later be known for proclaiming that war is "cruelty" and "War is Hell" was shaken by what he saw on his first battlefield, and it laid the foundation for his belief in the severity of war.

Sherman's three regiments were now spent and out of the fight. In fact, the entire Union army was exhausted and on the verge of collapse. By 3:45 P.M., McDowell had committed his last fresh brigade, commanded by Col. Oliver O. Howard, into the fight. Howard's four regiments had been greatly fatigued by a long march and lack of water. They were ordered to advance on the run, but one-fourth of their number fell out from thirst and exhaustion before reaching the battlefield. Howard formed his remaining men in two lines of battle and ordered the attack. His first line was badly mauled by Confederate fire and retreated from the field. Howard went back down the slope to personally lead his second line against the enemy. As Howard's second line ascended the slope, it met the same destructive fire that had greeted the first. In addition, there were fresh Confederate brigades forming on their right flank. The remainder of Joe Johnston's army from the Shenandoah Valley, under the command of Edmund Kirby Smith, had arrived on the field and was now prepared to seize victory for Southern arms. The sight of Confederate reinforcements seemed to take the fight out of Union troops that had fought and struggled for so many hours over this blood-soaked field. Howard said that "A panic seized all the troops in sight." Men began throwing away their muskets and making for the rear.

A large number of civilians had come out from Washington to witness this first great battle of the war. Many brought picnic lunches and approached the event as if it were a sporting enterprise instead of the scene of mortal combat. When McDowell's army began to retire from the field, the exodus of these thrill-seeking civilians served to clog the roads and create a traffic jam. When a Confederate shell burst in the middle of a bridge, overturning a wagon, just as two Union columns of soldiers arrived, all thought of an orderly retreat was abandoned. Fear and panic quickly spread throughout the Union army, until the organization of companies, regiments, and brigades dissolved into a chaotic mob of frightened and fleeing men. Shouts that Confederate cavalry was about to ride them down hastened the pace of the retreating men and civilians, and all joined in a rush toward Washington for safety. Many did not stop running until they had successfully reached the city limits.

In reality, the frenzied mob had little to fear from the victorious Confederates. Beauregard and Johnston had won the day, but it was not within reason for the Confederates to follow up their victory with an active pursuit of the defeated foe. The Confederates were nearly as disorganized and exhausted from the battle as the Federals and lacked the ability to follow up their victory. Union losses had been 2,896 in killed, wounded, and missing, of which 1,312 were captured. Southern losses were much lower, being only 1,982, but only 13 of that number were captured, meaning that the Confederates had actually suffered greater losses in killed and wounded. The first great battle of the war was ended. Cump had witnessed his first battlefield, and the Union had suffered the first of what would become a string of defeats. The South exalted in the victory, and most of the Southern people felt that one more victory was all that would be needed to secure Confederate independence. In the North, people tried to make sense of the defeat and came to the conclusion that greater efforts and sacrifice would be needed to restore the Union. With a soldier's simplicity, Sherman orders for his next assignment.

Chapter 8

ASSIGNED TO KENTUCKY

On August 7, 1861, the war department issued a promotion list for the army. Most of the ranking colonels who had led brigades at Manassas believed that they had no chance for promotion. Many, including Sherman, thought that they might be cashiered from the army due to the poor conduct of the troops in the recent battle. But Cump's name was among those being promoted, and he was elevated to the rank of brigadier general of volunteers. According to the date of promotion, he would be the Seventh ranking officer of that grade in the Union army. There was another new general of note in camp. On July 26, Maj. Gen. George B. McClellan had arrived in Washington. He had been summoned there by the war department to assume command of the army gathered in and around the city. McClellan's forces in western Virginia had won minor victories at Philippi and Rich Mountain, making him instantly a national hero, and he was hailed in the capital as the Union's Napoleon. Under McClellan's supervision, the wave of recruits flocking to Washington in response to Lincoln's call for three-year volunteers would be forged into the Army of the Potomac, one of the finest military organizations in history. Cump would have nothing to do with this army or its organization. His affiliation with the Eastern army was about to come to a close, and Sherman was soon to be headed west.

About a week after his promotion, Sherman received a note from Brig. Gen. Robert Anderson, requesting a meeting at the general's room at Willard's Hotel. When Cump met with Anderson he was informed that the latter had been placed in command of the Department of the Cumberland, encompassing the area of Kentucky and Tennessee. Anderson was given permission to choose four brigadier generals from the newly issued promotions list to assist him in the administration of his department. Having known Sherman and having gained a favorable estimation of his qualities when Cump had served as a subordinate officer at Fort Moultrie, Anderson made him one of his top choices. His other selections were George Henry Thomas, Don Carlos Buell, and Ambrose E. Burnside. When President Lincoln was hesitant to appoint Thomas, because he was from Virginia, and his loyalty to the Union was still in question, Sherman staunchly supported his old classmate, and, along with Anderson, he was able to convince the president to approve the assignment. Sherman also told Lincoln that he desired to serve in a subordinate position and did not want the responsibility of independent command. The president was amused by this statement, assuring Cump that there were enough officers who wanted high office that he did not think Sherman would be pressed into an unwanted command.

Several days later, Sherman was officially relieved of command with his brigade. The brigade was turned over to Brig. Gen. Fitz John Porter, and Sherman made his way to Cresson, Pennsylvania, where he met General Anderson and his family. The party then began a journey to Cincinnati, where they met General Thomas. The Department of the Cumberland existed more in name than in fact. Gen. Albert Sidney Johnston commanded the Confederate forces operating in the Western Theater. Johnston ordered Brig. Gen. Simon B. Buckner to cross into Kentucky from Tennessee and occupy the town of Bowling Green. Buckner entered Kentucky with a force of 5,000 men and took possession of the town on September 18. General Anderson devised that Louisville was probably Johnston's primary objective and took steps to counter that movement. The only problem was that Anderson had limited resources with which to make a response. Col. Lovell H. Rousseau had approximately 2,000 men, in camp opposite Louisville, but their organization was not yet completed, they had little or no training, and equipment was lacking. The Home Guard of Louisville, some 1,800 strong, was called out for 10 days' service. Anderson sent the Home Guard, under the command of Col. A. Y. Johnson, to Muldraugh's Hill, an escarpment halfway between Louisville and Elizabethtown, to establish a defensive line. A few hours later, Colonel Rousseau followed, with 1,200 men. Sherman was placed in overall command of the force.

On September 20, the Union position in Kentucky took a turn for the better when Col. B. F. Scribner arrived with the 38th Indiana Infantry. Four more Indiana regiments would soon follow. Most of the troops from the region had been funneled off to McClellan's army at Washington or Maj. Gen. John C. Fremont's army at St. Louis. Indiana Governor Oliver P. Morton had foresight to reserve a few regiments to guard against any potential situations that might arise in Kentucky, and these would now form the core of Anderson's force. Sherman did not find a position that suited him at Muldraugh's Hill, so he pushed on to Elizabethtown. Cump was in the process of establishing a line of defense at this point when he received a message from Gen. Winfield Scott. Anderson had been relieved of command, at his own request, by reason of failing health. Sherman, as the senior brigadier in the department, was ordered to assume overall command. Sherman did not want the job. "I am certain that, in my earliest communication to the War Department, I renewed the expression of my wish to remain in a subordinate position, and that I received the assurance that Brigadier General Buell would soon arrive from California, and would be sent to relieve me." This seemed to placate Cump. He was willing to serve as temporary commander until Buell completed the long journey from California, but he did not want it on a permanent basis.

The situation facing Cump was the same as had caused Anderson such physical and mental fatigue and led to his request to be relieved. Sherman had no staff to assist with the details of running the department and was forced to personally oversee all facets of command. He dutifully applied himself to the task, however. Working up to 20 hours a day, Sherman was raw energy in motion. He ate little and smoked cigars almost incessantly. Most of all, he worried. His department stretched for some 300 miles, and with only 20,000 men, Cump despaired of being able to defend this large expanse. He also believed wild reports and rumors about the size of the enemy force confronting him, placing the size of Albert Sidney Johnston's army at between two and five times his own. Men, arms, and supplies were hard to come by. McClellan, at Washington, and Fremont, at St. Louis, got top priority. The Department of the Cumberland received only what was left over. Sherman's troops were short of muskets, and many of those with which they had been armed were of inferior quality, including a large number of antiquated Belgian models.

The truth was that Johnston's army was about equal to Sherman's, and the Confederate commander was facing most of the same problems as Cump. Johnston was overestimating the numbers in Sherman's army and was informing Richmond that he was greatly outnumbered by Federal forces in the area. But Cump was convinced that he had been thrust into an untenable situation, and the responsibility of command began to weigh heavily on his mind. The first outward sign of his intense agitation and apprehension was seen in his dealings with members of the press. Sherman considered reporters to be worse than spies because of the fact that they frequently printed sensitive information about the army that was beneficial to the Confederates. Cump's normal disdain for the press turned to fear when he thought of how Johnston might make use of information concerning the weakness of his own command. In Sherman's mind, it became imperative that reporters were given no information, and he tried to expel all members of the press from his headquarters and the various army camps. When one reporter approached Sherman with a letter of introduction from Thomas Ewing Jr., the general read the note and then curtly instructed its carrier to make sure he was on the next train out of town. The reporter protested and told Cump that the citizens wanted news from the front, and he only wanted to be able to report the truth. Sherman exploded, "We don't want the truth told about things here—that's what we don't want! Truth, eh? No, sir! We don't want the enemy any better informed than he is." Sherman had reporters expelled from his camps and imprisoned one member of the press who had been denied a pass to go into the camp but decided to go in anyway.

Sherman's rough handling of reporters caused him to become a special target for the media. In the absence of facts, newspapers began to run vicious attacks on the general, most of them based on gossip and speculation. Sherman had strictly observed the property and individual rights of Southern sympathizers in Kentucky in order to keep from alienating those citizens of the Blue Grass state who had not yet made up their minds about which side to choose. His policy had beneficial results for the Union cause and influenced many Kentuckians in favor of the Union. Kentucky enlistments were approximately two Union volunteers for every one Confederate. Despite this fact, the newspapers proclaimed his soft attitude toward Southern sympathizers showed his disloyalty to the cause, hinting that he might be a traitor. Soon, rumors of Cump's own nervousness in regard to his military situation started to find their way into the newspaper columns. Sherman had been ill advised in voicing his opinions on the difficulties facing him and his subordinates, and rumors were rampant from those in the know in Louisville. One reporter stated that the general was almost overcome by the difficulties of his command and "could not rid himself of the apprehension that he was due for defeat if the rebels attacked." He also forwarded the secondhand information that Sherman paced the hallway outside his rooms at the Galt House for hours on end, and "guests whispered about him and the gossip was that he was insane."

On October 17, Sherman had a meeting with Secretary of War Simon Cameron. The secretary was accompanied by Adj. Gen. Lorenzo Thomas and several civilians. Sherman was anxious to plead his case for more men and equipment with Cameron, but was hesitant to speak of military matters in front of the civilians. The secretary assured him that he need not be concerned, as all members of the party could be trusted. Sherman flew into an excited explanation of the conditions within his department. He chastised the government for sending him 12,000 almost useless Belgian muskets with which to arm the Kentucky volunteers, and lobbied for the need of more troops in the department. Cump surprised the secretary by announcing that the Confederates could capture Louisville whenever they wanted. When Cameron asked how many men he felt were needed, Cump told him that a force of 60,000 would be required to defend Kentucky from the Confederates. In order to expel Albert Sidney Johnston's army from Kentucky, he told Cameron it would take, "before we are done, 200,000." The secretary was stunned by Sherman's statement and cried out, "Great God! Where are they to come from?" This would be twice the number of men Mc-Clellan had in the Army of the Potomac, protecting Washington.

The result of Sherman's interview with Cameron was that the war secretary thought him "unbalanced and that it would not do to leave him in command." General McClellan sent Col. T.M. Key to Louisville to investigate Sherman and report his findings. Key concluded that "Sherman was not sufficiently master of his judgment to warrant the intrusting to him of an important military command." Of more immediate import to the general was the fact that one of the civilians with Cameron at the time of their interview was a reporter, Samuel Wilkerson. Wilkerson worked for the *New York Tribune*, and his recounting of the meeting between Cameron and Sherman placed the general in the worst possible light, insinuating that Sherman was mentally unbalanced or insane. Other newspapers echoed these sentiments as the story spread throughout the North. Secretary Cameron had made the statement that Cump's request for 200,000 men was "insane," and that comment had been altered into Sherman himself being insane. Cameron allowed the reports to gain credence by refusing to step forward and set the record straight.

Sherman, of course, was not insane, but there was an element of truth in the reports the newspapers were spreading. The general was overwhelmed by the responsibilities of command. He had been sleeping little, eating less, and keeping a work schedule that would have exhausted a man half his age. Stress, fatigue, and apprehension had greatly agitated his mental state, causing him to be erratic in his judgment. Worry and exhaustion had driven Cump to the brink of a nervous breakdown. His detractors pointed to his odd behavior as proof that the general was stark raving mad.

Sherman refused to respond to the accusations made by the press. Instead, he drafted a report detailing the conditions in his department that was sent to Adj. Gen. Lorenzo Thomas on November 4. This report did little to improve Sherman's standing with the war department, or with George B. McClellan, who had recently been promoted to general-in-chief and given control over all the Union armies. Cump had merely reiterated his standing arguments that he was vastly outnumbered by the enemy, while his own troops were perfectly green and untrained. He had a lack of transportation for his troops, and the rail-

roads on which they depended were susceptible to sabotage by Southern sympathizers operating in his rear. His statement in the next to
last paragraph that no one comprehended the vastness of the enemy
army gathered before him, combined with his restating of the need for
200,000 men in his closing paragraph served to exemplify to his superiors that he had lost his grip on reality and was governed more by fear
than reason. At a time when most of the people in the country still
felt that the war would be relatively short in duration and would be a
minor affair in terms of the number of lives lost, Sherman stood alone
as a voice of impending doom. His predictions of a long and costly
war were contrary to popular opinion, and they served to promote the
idea that Cump had lost all grasp of reality. Neither McClellan nor
the war department probably thought that Sherman was insane, but
it was commonly held that he had been promoted to a position that
exceeded his abilities. Accordingly, on November 12, 1861, Cump was
relieved of command in the Department of the Cumberland and was
replaced by Maj. Gen. Don Carlos Buell, who had just arrived from
California. In reality, Buell was to have assumed the position upon
his arrival in Kentucky. Sherman's appointment to top command had
been only a temporary assignment. But instead of being a normal tran-
sition of power, Sherman's demotion now became a source of shame
and a serious blot on his service record. He had lost the confidence
of his superiors and had seemingly shown himself unsuited for high
command. Instead of being assigned to command a division within the
department, as should have been his right, Sherman was dispatched to
Missouri to train and organize new volunteers. McClellan was obvi-
ously crediting Colonel Key's report that Sherman was "not sufficiently
master of his judgment to warrant intrusting to him of an important
military command."

It took Sherman more than a week to prepare himself for relocation
to Missouri following his removal as department commander. During
this time, new regiments began pouring in to Louisville. Cump had
been crying for reinforcements, and now, at last, they were arriving.
By December, the total forces in the Department of the Cumberland
would amount to 100,000 men. Sherman had the opportunity to inspect several of the newly arrived regiments, but his spirits were not
buoyed by what he saw. Instead of being encouraged by their numbers,

he was depressed by their almost complete lack of training and discipline. Sherman saw these new volunteers as wide-eyed innocents, having no knowledge of the realities of war, and he feared for them when confronted with the savagery of the battlefield. In a letter dated November 21, 1861, he stated, "I cannot but look upon it as absolutely sacrificing them. I see no hope for them in their present raw and undisciplined condition, and some terrible disaster is inevitable. . . . I suppose I have been morose and cross and could I now hide myself in some obscure corner I would do so, for my conviction is that our Government is destroyed and no human power can restore it."

Insane or not, Sherman had lost confidence not only in himself, but also in the cause he supported. As such, he was no longer capable of performing as a commander of troops, and at that time, it seems as if McClellan and the war department was justified in reassigning him to a position where he could not hamper the war effort with his doom and gloom prophecy. In St. Louis, Sherman would be under the command of Maj. Gen. Henry W. Halleck, who had replaced Fremont in command of the Department of Missouri. Sherman found that the department was well staffed with troops, but observed that they were as poorly trained and equipped as the new regiments he had seen in Kentucky. The fear of coming disaster that gripped him in Kentucky surged forth again. When Halleck sent him to Sedalia to inspect the troops there, Cump was seized with anxiety over the disbursement of regiments commanded by Brig. Gen. John Pope. Sherman feared the units were too loosely connected and might be easily gobbled up by Confederate commander Maj. Gen. Sterling Price. He therefore issued orders for the various regiments to concentrate. Pope knew that Sterling Price had no intention of advancing upon his position and was confounded by Sherman's interference. He wired Halleck, in St. Louis, vehemently complaining about Cump's actions. Halleck ordered Sherman back to St. Louis, at once.

Sherman was, at this time, at the low point in his military career. Ellen had been seeing the despair in his letters and had been reading the articles published in the newspapers; she determined that her husband needed her support and encouragement. She hurried to St. Louis, arriving in the city just after Cump had departed for Sedalia. In an interview with Halleck, she had probably demanded that her husband be granted a furlough to go home and rest from his trying ordeal. The incident in Sedalia had convinced Halleck to grant this request. When Sherman arrived, he was surprised to see Ellen, and asked, "what are you doing here?" "I've come to bring you home," she calmly stated. Cump protested and asserted that his place was in St. Louis, but Halleck supported Ellen and told Cump that a 20-day rest would be good for him. Sensing that the decision had already been made, Sherman dutifully accompanied his wife back to Lancaster. In a letter to General McClellan, Halleck explained his decision to place Cump on leave, stating, "I am satisfied that General Sherman's physical and mental system is so completely broken by labor and care as to render him for the present unfit for duty. Perhaps a few weeks' rest may restore him. I am satisfied that in his present condition it would be dangerous to give him a command here."

The *Cincinnati Commercial* published a parting shot at the deposed commander, who greeted the general shortly after his arrival in Lancaster. "The painful intelligence reaches us in such form that we are not at liberty to discredit it, that General W.T. Sherman, late the Commander of the Department of the Cumberland is insane! It appears that he was at times, when commanding in Kentucky, stark mad. We learn that he at one time telegraphed to the War Department three times in one day for permission to evacuate Kentucky and retreat into Indiana. He also, on several occasions, frightened the leading Union men of Louisville almost out of their wits by the most astounding representations of the overwhelming force of Buckner, and the assertion that Louisville could not be defended. The retreat from Cumberland Gap was one of his mad freaks. When relieved of the command in Kentucky he was sent to Missouri and placed at the head of a brigade at Sedalia, when the shocking fact that he was a madman was developed by orders that his subordinates knew to be preposterous and refused to obey. He has of course been relieved altogether from command. The harsh criticisms which have been lavished upon this gentleman, provoked by his strange conduct, will now give way to feelings of the deepest sympathy for him in his great calamity. It seems providential that the country has not to mourn the loss of an army through the loss of the mind of a General into whose hands were committed the vast responsibilities of the command in Kentucky."

Sherman as a major general in the Union Army. (Library of Congress)

Not trusted by his superiors, shunned by his colleagues, and ridiculed in the press, Sherman's military career was in a shambles, and it seemed as if nothing could be done to salvage it. He had dedicated himself to the performance of his duty and had worked tirelessly to accomplish his assignment, but the result had been failure and shame. He had once referred to himself as a "vagabond." Could it be that he was to end his days in fruitless pursuit of the success he so greatly desired? The 20-day furlough he had been granted was intended as a time for Sherman to relax and refresh himself, but with questions like these crowding his thoughts it is doubtful if the time in Lancaster furnished the desired results. In the depths of despair, Sherman would later admit that he contemplated suicide while in Lancaster, and it was only the thought of his children that prevented him from taking his own life. As Cump looked to the future with sad apprehension he could little know that his star was about to ascend and that he was destined to arise from the ashes of his current circumstances like the phoenix.

Chapter 9

SHILOH AND A CAREER RESURRECTED

Sherman had been forsaken by many of his comrades in arms. Many friends and acquaintances from the old army believed Cump's recent difficulties made him too much of a liability for their own career advancement, and he might have spent the remainder of the war assigned to duty in some demeaning position far beneath his abilities or rank. Henry Halleck was not among this number. Halleck, with a lawyer's mind, had concluded that his luckless subordinate had a great deal to offer a commander willing to take a chance on him. Cump was well connected, politically, while Halleck had no influential champions of his own in the government. The influence that John Sherman and Thomas Ewing could exert on Halleck's behalf, as present and former U.S. senators, could significantly alter Halleck's own advancement possibilities. For the moment, Don Carlos Buell and Halleck were equals. One of them would inevitably be named the overall commander of the Western Theater, and Buell seemed to have the edge. He was a favorite of General McClellan, whose influence was considerable. Halleck needed his own supporters and saw Cump's influential family members as a means to an end.

Halleck cultivated a relationship with Sherman when he reported for duty following his leave and increasingly took Cump into his confidence in matters of military strategy and planning. In short order, Sherman became Halleck's closest confidant and his most trusted subordinate. Cump was part of a planning session held at Halleck's headquarters when the general was examining a map upon which had been drawn a line to show the position of Albert Sidney Johnston's army in Tennessee and Kentucky. Halleck asked where Cump thought the Confederate line was the most vulnerable, and Sherman responded that he thought the center of the Southern line was weakest. Halleck traced a line down the map with his finger to the Cumberland and Tennessee Rivers and proclaimed that this should be the proper line of operations for an offensive against Johnston. One month later, Ulysses S. Grant initiated his campaign against Forts Henry and Donelson on the Tennessee and Cumberland Rivers.

In the meantime, Sherman had been assigned to command the military post at Paducah, Kentucky. Paducah served as a vital link in Grant's supply line, and Sherman played a key role in making sure that Grant's men received the supplies and war material they needed to carry out the campaign. Cump enthusiastically threw himself into his work and saw to it that Grant's army wanted for nothing. Although he was Grant's superior in rank, he conducted himself as if he were under Grant's orders, and concerned himself only with the success of the mission. Grant would later write that "every boat that came up with supplies or reinforcements brought a note of encouragement from Sherman, asking me to call upon him for any assistance he could render and saying that if he could be of service at the front I might send for him and he would waive rank." The cordial relations that began with their association in the campaign against Forts Henry and Donelson were to blossom into a lifelong friendship, based in mutual admiration and trust. Grant's expedition captured Fort Henry on February 6, 1862. Fort Donelson fell 10 days later. Albert Sidney Johnston's line was broken, and the Confederate army withdrew from Kentucky and Tennessee, uncovering the important cities of Nashville and Memphis to Union capture. The decisive action had taken place in Halleck's theater of operations, and he reaped the spoils of the victory by being named as commander of all Union forces operating in the Western Theater.

Halleck should have been thankful to Grant for providing him with the victory necessary to gain his promotion but quite the opposite was true. Halleck began complaining to the war department about Grant's failure to file reports, or to even answer communications he received from headquarters. Halleck went so far as to speculate that Grant had once more fallen into the habits that had gotten him discharged from the army prior to the war: drunkenness. Halleck relieved Grant of command, and placed Brig. Gen. Charles F. Smith in his place at the head of the Army of the Tennessee. Back in Washington, Grant soon discovered that he had a friend in the government. Abraham Lincoln sifted through the details of the case and decided that Grant had been the architect of the victories at Henry and Donelson. The president determined that he might be a bit shoddy when it came to filling out reports and following military protocol, but he was not afraid to fight. Lincoln decided to intervene on Grant's behalf. Instead of shelving this general, as Halleck desired, the president had him promoted to the rank of major general.

The Confederate army withdrew to Corinth, Mississippi, in the northern portion of the state, where General Johnston attempted to reorganize his forces and plan his next movement against the Federals. Halleck gave Sherman, the assignment of leading the advance of the army in pursuit of the Confederates. Sherman was given the task of leading a division ordered to tear up the tracks of the Memphis and Charleston Railroad. Cump's division was transported by boat, landing near Burnsville, where the command disembarked and prepared to destroy the railroad shops and depots within the town. Heavy rains had swollen local streams into raging torrents, and several men of Sherman's command died by drowning in the rushing waters. Flood waters inundated the surrounding countryside, and Sherman determined that further movement toward Burnsville was impossible. Ordering his men back aboard the ships, the division traveled up the Tennessee River, arriving at Pittsburgh Landing on March 14, where he planned to disembark his men and make another attempt at breaking the railroad. Leaving the troops aboard the transports, Cump made his way to Savannah, where General Smith had established his headquarters, to report on his recent activities. Smith directed Sherman to disembark his men at Pittsburgh Landing, along with the division of Brig. Gen.

Stephen A. Hurlburt. Smith ordered Sherman to make sure both divisions took up positions well back from the landing, so as to allow room for the rest of the army once it arrived. Sherman allowed his men to stay aboard the ships for several days, not disembarking them until March 19, when he "took a post about three miles back, three of the brigades covering the roads to Purdy and Corinth, and the other brigade (Stuart's) temporarily at a place on the Hamburg Road, near Lick Creek Ford, where the Bark Road came into the Hamburg Road." Over the next few days, the divisions of Maj. Gens. Benjamin M. Prentiss, John McClernand, William H. L Wallace, and Lew Wallace arrived and were positioned on the field. Lew Wallace's division was placed on the far right of the Union line, on the opposite shore of Snake Creek, in a position not really connected with the rest of the army. Prentiss's division was formed on Sherman's left, with the divisions of Hurlburt, McClernand, and W.H.L. Wallace taking positions behind Sherman and Prentiss, nearer the landing.

Ulysses S. Grant rejoined the army on March 17. Charles Smith had been incapacitated from a leg injury sustained while jumping into a rowboat. He received a minor cut, but infection set in and would eventually lead to his death on April 25, 1862. With Smith unable to exercise the responsibilities of command, Grant had been reinstated to lead the Army of the Tennessee. Grant approved the dispositions Sherman had made and left him nominally in command of the encampment before removing to Savannah, some 12 miles distant, where he took over the headquarters Smith had established.

Grant's army numbered more than 40,000 men. According to intelligence he had received, Johnston's Confederate army at Corinth numbered only about 20,000. Grant credited this information and felt that Johnston would not risk his army by taking the offensive against a force twice the size of his own. Instead, Grant expected the Confederates to fortify their position at Corinth in hopes of being able to defend their works against the larger Federal army. In reality, Johnston's numbers were about equal to Grant's, and the Confederate was planning just the sort of offensive operation Grant was discounting. Johnston learned that Don Carlos Buell's Army of the Ohio was marching to join Grant at Pittsburgh Landing. When Buell arrived, the combined Federal armies would have the numerical superiority Grant believed he now held, and Johnston knew that he could not hope to win a battle against these odds. His only option was to attack Grant and hopefully defeat his army before Buell arrived. If he could take on the Federal armies one at a time, he might still have a chance for victory.

On April 3, Johnston marched his army, some 44,000 strong, out of Corinth, pointing them in the direction of Pittsburgh Landing. It took two days for Johnston's army to cover the 20 miles between Corinth and Pittsburgh Landing because the march was impeded by heavy rain. By April 5, the Confederates were within two miles of the Union encampments, and their movement had not yet been detected. When a number of the green troops in the ranks fired off their muskets to make sure their powder had not been damaged by the rain, Gen. P.G.T. Beauregard, Johnston's second in command, felt that the Federals must have been alerted to the danger lurking in front of them and argued against making an attack the following morning. Johnston's mind was made up, however, and he stuck to his decision to launch the assault early the next day.

Beauregard's concerns proved to be unfounded. The Federals were blissfully unaware that a Confederate army was massed in their front. Reports had been coming in from pickets of enemy activity in the front, but the Union high command discounted this as merely some detachments of Southern cavalry. In his memoirs, Sherman states that the pickets had made contact with Confederates, "but thus far we had not positively detected the presence of infantry." Even the discharge of Confederate artillery was dismissed as being nothing more than horse artillery that accompanied the cavalry. When an Ohio colonel told Sherman that he was sure an enemy attack was imminent, Cump lashed out, yelling "Take your damned regiment back to Ohio. There is no enemy nearer than Corinth." Grant concurred in Sherman's assessment of the situation. On the night of April 5, he telegraphed General Halleck, "I have scarcely the faintest of an attack (general one) being made upon us."

At 5:15 a.m., on the morning of April 6, a reconnaissance from the 25th Missouri made contact with Confederate outposts and a sharp firefight ensued. This finally convinced Sherman that something might be wrong in his front and he ordered his men to arms. He also ordered a battery of artillery posted at Shiloh Church, the Methodist structure that would lend its name to the battle. At 6:00 A.M., Johnston formed his army in line of battle with Maj. Gen. Leonidus Polk's corps on the left, Maj. Gen. Braxton Bragg's corps in the center, and Maj. Gen. William J. Hardee's corps on the right. Maj. Gen. John C. Breckinridge's corps was held in reserve. By 8:00 A.M., the Confederate battle line fell like a hammer on Sherman's division, as well as Prentiss's division, on Sherman's left. Prentiss was doing his best to withstand the pressure from the Confederate assault, but when the enemy overlapped his line and began attacking his division on both flanks, as well as in front, his whole division soon broke for the rear. Prentiss was able to rally about 1,000 of his men and placed them in the center of a new defensive line being formed by Generals Hulrburt and W.H.L. Wallace. This new line proved to be formidable, being in a densely wooded area along an old sunken road. Fighting raged in this area throughout the morning and into the afternoon, as 11 different Confederate attacks were repulsed. The fighting along this line was so intense, and the bullets were flying so thick that the men soon dubbed this part of the battlefield the Hornet's Nest.

Sherman, now supported by McClernand, was still making a stubborn stand around Shiloh Church. The Confederates massed their artillery against this portion of the Union line, attempting to bombard the Federals into submission. Grant had been roused by the first sounds of the battle and immediately boarded a ship to take him to Pittsburgh Landing. Along the way, he had the steamer swing close in to Crump's Landing to yell out orders to Lew Wallace to be prepared to act on any directions he might receive from Grant to support the engaged divisions. Upon arriving at Pittsburgh Landing, Grant made his way to Shiloh Church to confer with Sherman, arriving there about 10:00 A.M. Sherman and McClernand had withstood the Confederate assault for approximately two hours, by this time, and Grant plainly saw that the troops were about fought out, and the line could not hold much longer. He issued orders for Lew Wallace to bring his division onto the field, to support Sherman and McClernand before moving down the line to check on Hulrburt, Prentiss, and W.H.L. Wallace.

But Lew Wallace's division did not appear on the field. He took a different road than the one Grant intended, which delayed his arrival. Without reinforcement from Lew Wallace, Sherman was pushed back from his position along Shiloh Church Ridge, and he was finally able to re-establish his line to the right of the defensive position held by Hurlburt, Prentiss, and W.H.L. Wallace. When Lew Wallace finally did reach Shiloh Church he found that Sherman had already withdrawn and that his division was now in the rear of the Confederate army. Wallace would later state that he was in a perfect position from which to launch an attack against the exposed rear of Johnston's army, but that orders from Grant directed him to join the rest of the Federal army near Pittsburgh Landing. Wallace retraced his steps back to Crump's Landing and then set out to join Grant's main body. The end result was that Wallace's division marched back and forth on the battlefield for the entire day and did not reach Pittsburgh Landing until that evening, having taken no part in the fighting.

As Sherman's line was falling back, "the enemy's cavalry charged us, but were handsomely repulsed by the Twenty-ninth Illinois Regiment. The Fifth Ohio Battery, which had come up, rendered good service in holding the enemy in check for some time, and Major Taylor also came up with another battery and got into position, just in time to get a good flank fire upon the enemy's column, as he pressed on General McClernand's right, checking his advance; when General McClernand's division made a fine charge on the enemy and drove him back into the ravines to our front and right. I had a clear field, about two hundred yards wide, in my immediate front, and contented myself with keeping the enemy's infantry at that distance during the rest of the day." Sherman was indeed holding his own on the right side of the Union line, but things were not going as well for Prentiss, Hurlburt, and W.H.L. Wallace.

The Hornet's Nest had been the most hotly contested part of the battlefield ever since Prentiss had been forced back from his original line of battle. The Confederates threw themselves at the Union defenders of the sunken road in charge after charge, but the blue-clad troops repulsed every attempt to oust them from their stronghold. Meanwhile, General Johnston observed that the Union army was being driven straight back, toward their base of supplies at Pittsburgh Landing. Johnston had intended to turn the left flank of the Federal army and drive it away from the landing, cutting it off from its supplies and avenue of escape, and forcing it into the swampy ground around

Snake and Owl Creeks. At approximately 12:00 P.M., Johnston took personal command of the right flank of his army and organized another charge, which he led in person. This assault succeeded in driving back the Federal left for about three-fourths of a mile. Johnston's lines had become intermingled, and the assault was halted so the men could reform for another attack. Johnston was mounted on his horse, supervising the organization, when he was struck in the leg by a bullet. Suffering a severed artery, Johnston bled to death because no surgeon was at hand, and none of his officers knew anything about applying a tourniquet that would have saved his life. Johnston died at approximately 2:30 P.M., and his death caused active operations on the Confederate right to cease for about an hour.

General Beauregard assumed command of the army as soon as he was informed of the death of Johnston. Beauregard sent Bragg to the right to assume command of the flank that Johnston had been supervising, and directed Brig. Gen. Daniel Ruggles to take charge of the Confederate center, operating against the Hornet's Nest. Ruggles had been present for the 11 bloody repulses that had thus far marked the efforts of the Confederates at the Hornet's Nest. Realizing that infantry alone could not move the Federals from their position, Ruggles ordered all the artillery he could find, 62 pieces, gathered in front of the Union center. The Confederate big guns were unloosed upon the Hornet's Nest with devastating effect. The Federals were taking heavy casualties from the bombardment, and Ruggles sensed that that their line was beginning to waiver. Ruggles then sent in his infantry, and the Union line broke. The units to the left and right of Prentiss and Wallace retreated toward the landing, and the Confederates swirled around these isolated troops and encircled them. W.H.L. Wallace ordered his troops to withdraw, but his men had to pass through a ravine that was already a gauntlet of fire. Wallace was killed while making the attempt, and only two of his regiments were successful in eluding the trap. Prentiss, with the remnant of his division and the remainder of Wallace's division, made a gallant stand against the Confederates who were now assaulting the Hornet's Nest from all directions. By 5:30 P.M., Prentiss and his survivors had withstood all that men could take, and the 2,200 remaining men from these two divisions were compelled to surrender.

Sherman's division had been receiving rough treatment as well. The Confederates captured Sherman's camps and had forced his battle line to give ground on several occasions, but the division was still in the fight and was contesting every inch of ground. The determined stand of his men must have caused Cump great pride. "My division was made up of regiments perfectly new, nearly all having received their muskets for the first time at Paducah. None of them had ever been under fire or beheld heavy columns of an enemy bearing down on them." New to the service, and with almost no training, these men were responding to the Confederate assaults with grit and determination. Not all of the men stood fast, however, but Sherman made allowance for those who left the ranks to seek safety back at the landing. "To expect of them the coolness and steadiness of older troops would be wrong. They knew not the value of combination and organization. When individual fears seized them, the first impulse was to get away."

Sherman was displaying a great amount of grit and determination as well. Exposing himself to the worst of the fire, he seemed to be everywhere, directing and encouraging his men. Over the course of the battle, he would have four horses shot from under him and would have a piece of buckshot go through one of his hands. Cump's wound did not distract his attention from the fighting. He calmly took a handkerchief and wrapped the wound, without taking his eyes off the enemy, and then placed the hand inside his tunic, next to his breast. A second Rebel bullet tore one of his shoulder straps, grazing his skin. When one of General Grant's aides sought Cump out to inquire how the battle was going on his part of the field, Sherman responded, "Tell Grant if he has any men to spare I can use them; if not, I will do the best I can. We are holding them pretty well just now-pretty well-but it's as hot as hell." Hell was an accurate analogy. The air seemed to be filled with death, and the ground, in all directions, was littered with the dead and wounded. The Union troops were fighting with a resolve far greater than that normally seen in raw soldiers, but they were being pushed back all along the line. Sherman seemed to all who observed him on the battlefield to be the model of composure and calmness. His usually restless and excited nature was so engrossed with the business at hand that he exuded a relaxed and confident attitude to his men. One newspaper reporter stated, "All around him were excited orderlies and officers, but though his face was besmeared with powder and blood, battle seemed to have cooled his usually hot nerves."

In the late afternoon, General Grant took actions to safeguard his army and prepare a strong defensive line in the event his forces were completely swept from the battlefield. Grant ordered a number of heavy siege artillery brought up and placed in line one-half mile from the landing. Field artillery was placed on either end of this line. All of this firepower would be supported by the big naval cannon of the gunboats, anchored in the Tennessee River. Should his lines give way, Grant was sure that he would have a strong and defensible line upon which he could rally his troops and repulse any attack the Confederates might make. He need not have worried about fending off further Southern assaults, though. General Beauregard was of the opinion that his army had accomplished enough for one day. Beauregard was convinced that General Buell's Army of the Ohio was still too distant from Pittsburgh Landing to be of any assistance to Grant, so he determined to call off any more attacks until the next morning. He would give his men an opportunity to eat and rest for the night before finishing Grant off. But Beauregard had been badly misinformed. The lead elements of Buell's army arrived at Savannah by the evening of April 5. By the first day of the battle there were 17,000 men from the Army of the Ohio in the vicinity, and on the night of April 6 and the early morning of April 7, the Navy was busy transporting these fresh men across the river. When Morning dawned on April 7, the Confederates would be facing not only the survivors of Grant's army, but also nearly half of Buell's army.

Cump had seen Grant and Buell on the evening of April 6 and had learned from them the general situation on the field. Lew Wallace had finally arrived from Crump's Landing, and his division was formed to the right and rear of Sherman's. Buell's forces were extending Grant's line to the left as they ferried across the river. Grant had given orders for the Union forces to attack as soon as daylight dawned, believing that the first side to strike would emerge victorious in the battle. At 5:00 A.M., the Union line moved forward, with the divisions of Buell's Army of the Ohio, on the left, leading the way. Lew Wallace's division, on the right of the line, was the first to make contact with the enemy. One lone Southern brigade attempted to make a stand against

Union troops being attacked in their camps during the opening of the battle of Shi-loh. The stand made by Sherman's troops on the first day greatly enabled a Union victory on the second day of fighting. (U.S. Military History Institute)

Wallace's advance, but was soon overpowered and forced to retire a dis-tance of a mile. On the left, Buell's men were advancing so rapidly that they outdistanced their artillery support. When they finally did make contact with the main line of the Confederates, near a peach orchard, the Federals were repulsed by a furious counterattack. By this time, Sherman was in a position to watch the men of Col. August Willich's 32nd Indiana Infantry charge the enemy and be repulsed. Sherman wrote, "here I saw for the first time the well-ordered and compact col-umns of General Buell's Kentucky forces, whose soldierly movements at once gave confidence to our newer and less disciplined men. Here I saw Willich's regiment advance upon a point of water-oaks and thicket, behind which I knew the enemy was in great strength, and enter it in beautiful style. Then arose the severest musketry-fire I ever heard, and lasted some twenty minutes, when this splendid regiment had to fall back."

By 2:00 P.M., Buell's men reformed their lines and pushed forward another assault. Brig. Gen. Lovell Rousseau's brigade formed for the attack, and Sherman placed two of his brigades in line to Rousseau's right. Cump procured two 24-pound howitzers, and personally directed the fire of these guns against two Confederate batteries that had been inflicting damage on the Union line. The three brigades swept forward, and though the Confederates launched a series of countercharges, the Union forces were driving the enemy steadily backward. Sherman's troops kept up the pressure on the retiring Southerners, despite the fact that many of his troops had run out of ammunition. It was customary for a regiment that had expended all of its ammunition to retire from the field to replenish its cartridge boxes, but Sherman "appealed to regiments to stand fast, although out of cartridges . . . because to retire a regiment for any cause has a bad effect on others. I commend the Fortieth Illinois and Thirteenth Missouri for thus holding their ground under heavy fire, although their cartridge boxes were empty." By 4:00 P.M., the Federal line had pushed forward to the point that is had recovered all the ground lost to the Confederates on the previous day. General Beauregard determined that further fighting would be a useless waste of his soldier's lives and gave orders for his commanders to disengage from the fighting and begin a retreat toward Corinth. Union forces seemed content to have recaptured the camps lost on the previous day and no effort was made to pursue the enemy. Grant later stated that his army was too disorganized and exhausted to contemplate such a movement.

On Tuesday, April 8, the division of Brig. Gen. Thomas Wood, accompanied by Sherman and two of his brigades, with the Fourth Illinois Cavalry, set out in pursuit of Beauregard's army. The Federals caught up with the Confederate rearguard six miles south of Shiloh, at Fallen Timbers. Col. Nathan Bedford Forrest was in command of the rearguard, and he flung his cavalry on the lead elements of the pursuit, scattering the Federal skirmish line and throwing the cavalry into confusion. Forrest's cavalry pushed on until it made contact with the Union main body. Outnumbered and overmatched, the Southern horsemen were easily repulsed, and Forrest was badly wounded in the side, but his audacity in attacking a force several times the size of his own had the effect of discouraging any further Federal pursuit. Sherman and Wood returned to the camps around Shiloh. The Shiloh Campaign came to an end.

The battle of Shiloh was considered by most of the men who battled there to be the most terrible fighting they witnessed during the entire war.

Although other later battles saw greater numbers of total casualties, the percentage of loss at Shiloh would seem to bear out the impression of the combatants who fought there. The North suffered 13,047 total casualties, as compared to 10,699 for the Confederates, for a total of 23,746. When one considers the numbers of men engaged, this breaks down to 280 out of every 1,000 Federal soldiers engaged being killed or wounded, and 225 out of every 1,000 Confederate troops engaged being hit.

Sherman's performance at Shiloh had been exemplary. Only a few months before, he had been accused of being insane and had been removed from command under a cloud that threatened to end his military career. Now, he was being praised for his leadership and ability. In his official report, Grant praised Cump for his "great judgment and skill" and said, "To his individual efforts, I am indebted for the success of that battle." General Halleck informed the war department, "It is the unanimous opinion here that Brig. Gen. W.T. Sherman saved the fortune of the day on the 6th instance, and contributed largely to the glorious victory on the 7th. He was in the thickest of the fight on both days." Halleck recommended Cump's service be rewarded with a promotion to the rank of major general of volunteers. Sherman's promotion was confirmed unanimously, and he was appointed to rank on May 1, 1862.

While Sherman's star was ascending, Grant's was falling to earth. The general was being assailed from all sides for his handling of the army during the battle. Newspapers that had recently been calling for Cump's dismissal now turned their attention to Grant and proclaimed him unfit for command. The prevailing opinion was that Grant had allowed his army to be surprised at Shiloh, and it was only through the courageous efforts of men like Sherman that the army had not been destroyed. General Halleck apparently agreed with the public opinion, for when he arrived at Pittsburgh Landing, he relieved Grant from command of the Army of Tennessee and replaced him with George Henry Thomas. Grant was assigned to be Halleck's second in command, a position with little authority and no responsibility. Although he had not been dismissed from the army, Halleck had effectively removed Grant from command.

Sherman had compassion for Grant. He had faced similar circumstances in Kentucky and knew what Grant was going through. When

Cump heard that Grant was planning to leave the army, he went to talk to him. Sherman had a long, passionate discussion with Grant, in which he pointed out that quite recently he had lost faith in himself and had contemplated leaving the army. Shiloh had proved to be a change of fortunes for him, and now he was "in fine feather." If Grant left, that would be the end of it. He would be remembered only as a failure. If he stayed, the opportunity might present itself that would allow him to redeem his career and show the world his true ability. Cump's argument proved successful, and by the time the two officers parted he had received Grant's word that he would stay in the army, at least for a while longer, and he would not leave without first talking to Sherman. Cump had been instrumental in keeping Grant in the army, and without his intervention the services of this officer might have been lost to the Union. Sherman was, at this time, also responsible for starting another officer who would become famous on the road to advancement. Capt. Philip Sheridan had just returned to the army from service in the West, and Sherman at once began soliciting his advancement. Cump made various inquiries on Sheridan's behalf, in an effort to secure a regimental command, which eventually paid off when Sheridan was appointed colonel of the Second Michigan Cavalry. Many future historians would cite Grant, Sherman, and Sheridan as being the three greatest Union commanders to fight in the Civil War, and Sherman had played a prominent role in the creation of this triumvirate.

Chapter 10

VICKSBURG

Following the Union victory at Shiloh, General Halleck brought together the resources of the Western Theater at Pittsburgh Landing to
embark on a campaign to capture Corinth and destroy the Confederate army. Halleck would succeed in building an army of approximately
120,000 men with which to undertake this venture, and he would outnumber the Confederate army at Corinth by two-to-one. Despite this
numerical advantage, Halleck moved forward slowly and cautiously.
He was not about to be taken by surprise, as he felt Grant had been at
Shiloh. The army moved only a couple miles a day and would then stop
to throw up elaborate field works for defense against attack. So slow
were Halleck's movements that it took his army three weeks to march
the final five miles to the destination of Corinth. Sherman used this
time to drill and train the men in his division. He had been impressed
with the discipline and soldierly bearing of the troops in Buell's command on the field of Shiloh and sought to transform his own citizen
volunteers into veteran troops. Part of his disciplinary training came in
the form of instructing his men on how to conduct themselves while
operating in enemy territory. Strict orders were issued prohibiting
soldiers in his command from violating the rights or private property

of citizens along their line of march, and on more than one occasion he was seen to personally expel from private property. Looting from Southern homes was to be punished just as if it had taken place in the North, and the security of noncombatants was to be preserved. Cump was making war on the Southern military, not on Southern civilians, and he would not tolerate any soldier in his command who deviated from this policy. Many of his soldiers must have looked back upon this time with irony when they followed him in the March to the Sea, and participated in the program of total war that Sherman waged on Georgia two years later.

By May 25, Halleck army was at the gates of Corinth, and preparations were made to lay siege to the town. General Beauregard realized that his army could not withstand a siege of the town, and he planned his withdrawal toward Tupelo. Beauregard ordered three days' rations to be issued to his men, with instructions that they were to prepare for a battle. This was done in an effort to confuse Halleck. Beauregard knew that some of his men might desert to the Federals and would inform their captors that the Confederates were preparing for a fight. The ruse worked perfectly, and instead of attacking the Southern works, Halleck placed his artillery and planned his siege tactics, thus buying Beauregard several days to gather transportation and make good his withdrawal. On the night of May 29, Beauregard evacuated his army using trains on the Mobile and Ohio Railroad. Every time a train rolled into town it was greeted with cheers from the troops to convince the Federals that reinforcements were arriving. In reality, Beauregard's men were boarding the trains and leaving town. By the morning of May 30, all the Confederates were gone, along with most of their artillery and supplies. Corinth had been left undefended, and elements of Sherman's command moved forward to take control of the town.

The capture of Corinth served to further enhance the reputation of General Halleck, despite the fact that he had inflicted no damage on the Confederate army. He was called east to assume the position of general-in-chief of all Union armies and to assist the war department in the persecution of the war. This change provided General Grant the opportunity Sherman had promised would come, as Grant was reinstated in command of the Army of the Tennessee.

The transfer of Halleck meant that there was no longer a single officer in overall command in the Western Theater. Grant's Army of the Tennessee and Buell's Army of the Ohio would work independently of one another and confine their activity to within the limits of the military departments assigned to them. Before departing for Washington, Halleck saw to it that Cump received a choice assignment by appointing him to command the garrison in Memphis, Tennessee, with his division. Sherman arrived in the city on July 21 to assume military command of Memphis and its surroundings. The city had fallen into virtual anarchy after its evacuation by Confederate forces, and unsavory elements terrorized the citizenry. Among his first acts was to reinstate the local police force and to support the mayor and other local officials in the administration of their offices. Although civil authority was restored, Sherman made sure that no resident of Memphis failed to realize that the city was under military rule. In order to combat the lawlessness and to bring an end to guerrilla activity, Sherman adopted a number of harsh measures toward the citizens of Memphis that were far different than those he had enforced on the march to Corinth.

Sherman also used his troops, along with slave labor, appropriated from the surrounding plantations, to construct a series of strong works around the city. His belief was that Memphis would become an important supply depot for operations further south once Grant undertook active campaigning once more, and it would be absolutely necessary that the place be easily defended against any enemy efforts to retake it. For the time being, however, no offensive operations were in the offing, and Grant's army was assuming a defensive posture in western Tennessee. This was as a result of the Army of the Tennessee being temporarily under strength. General Buell was conducting a campaign against Chattanooga, in the eastern part of the state, where he was opposed by General Braxton Bragg's Army of Tennessee. The Confederate government had recently passed the Conscription Act, and the ranks of Bragg's army had been swelled by the first batch of draftees. Buell, facing a Confederate army of ever-increasing size, appealed to Grant for reinforcements from his army, compelling Grant to act on the defensive and merely protect the ground his army already occupied until such time as his units could be returned. Sherman would spend all of the summer and most of the fall supervising the military command of Memphis, while Grant waited to once more have the manpower to assume an offensive against the enemy.

In October 1862, a portion of Grant's army thwarted a Confederate attempt to recapture Corinth, Mississippi. Maj. Gen. Earl Van Dorn led a Southern force of approximately 22,000 men against Maj. Gen. William S. Rosecrans 23,000 Union defenders. In two days of desperate fighting, the Union forces were finally able to drive off the Confederates and force Van Dorn to retreat to Holly Springs, Mississippi. The battle of Corinth had the effect of placing Grant's army on the offensive again. In November, Grant ordered Sherman to meet him in Columbus, Kentucky to discuss plans for a winter campaign.

Grant's army occupied a line extending from Memphis, Tennessee to Corinth, Mississippi. What Grant proposed was to move on the Confederate army in the vicinity of Holly Springs, now under the newly promoted Lt. Gen. John C. Pemberton, who had been assigned to command the Department of Mississippi and West Louisiana on October 10. Grant, with a portion of his army, was at Oxford, Mississippi. He proposed to hold Pemberton's Confederates in check while Sherman mounted an expedition from Memphis, designed to capture Vicksburg and open navigation of the Mississippi River all the way to New Orleans.

The date set for Sherman to begin his expedition was December 18, but a shortage of available transports for his troops forced the starting date back to December 20. Sherman departed Memphis with three divisions, numbering more than 30,000 men. In addition, he was to be joined by a division from Helena, Arkansas, making his attack force more than 40,000 strong. On Christmas Eve, Cump's force arrived at Milliken's Bend, where a portion of Brig. Gen. Andrew J. Smith's division was landed the following day for the purpose of destroying track on the Vicksburg and Texas Railroad. Sherman advanced his main body down the river, and landed the division of Brig. Gen. Morgan L. Smith across from the mouth of the Yazoo River, with orders to tear up the tracks at that point.

On December 26, Sherman steamed his command 12 miles up the Yazoo River, accompanied by Porter's Navy gunboats. On December 27, he ordered his force be landed on the south bank of the Yazoo, near the mouth of Chickasaw Bayou. The spot selected for the landing was really more of an island than anything else, a densely wooded piece of ground surrounded by swamps and quicksand. Sherman had more than 30,000 troops with him. The Confederates, commanded by Maj. Gen. Stephen D. Lee, had fewer than 14,000 men. But the defenders held a great advantage in the strength of their position. They had positioned themselves along a steep line of ridges known as Chickasaw Bluffs. On December 27, Sherman probed the Confederate defenses, looking for a weakness, and the following day he ordered Brig. Gen. Frederick Steele's division to attempt to turn the Confederate right flank. The nature of the ground meant that Steele would have to attack over a narrow front, and he was easily repulsed by the Confederates. Sherman ordered a general assault to be made on December 29. His entire line was to engage the enemy, while an attempt to cross the Chickasaw Bayou was made a two points. Sherman's troops made a gallant assault, following a four-hour artillery bombardment, and through weight of numbers succeeded in capturing the advance line of Confederate rifle pits. The attack faltered when it came in contact with the main line of Southern defenses, where the Union troops were greeted with a hail of fire from small arms and cannon. The Northern troops wavered, then fell back. General Lee ordered a countercharge, and the Confederate troops pushed forward to capture 332 of the fleeing Federals and four battle flags. Cump had planned two more attacks, but the impregnable appearance of the Confederate defenses, combined with the fact that Admiral Porter could not bring the heavy cannon aboard his gunboats to bear on the scene of fighting caused him to call off any further efforts. On January 2, 1863, Sherman re-embarked his troops and returned to Milliken's bend.

The expedition had proved to be a failure. Union losses totaled 1,176 in killed, wounded, and captured, as opposed to only 187 casualties suffered by the Confederates, making it one of the most lop-sided battles to be fought during the war. The one-sided results of the campaign were used by reporters to show that it was an ill-advised venture, and they soon revived reports that Sherman was insane in the stories sent to their papers. Part of the reason for the failure was the strong position occupied by Lee's Confederates, and part lay in the difficult nature of the ground on which Sherman was operating. But the expedition was to have been aided by strong reinforcements from Grant's wing of the army, and this assistance never materialized. Grant's plans were altered due to the capture of Holly Springs, on December 20, by Confederate forces under the command of Maj. Gen. Earl Van Dorn. The loss of his supply depot, along with the 1,500 troops that had garrisoned it, caused Grant to change his plans regarding the immediate capture of Vicksburg while he looked to safeguarding his own line of supplies to the rear of the army. This delay gave General Pemberton the time he needed to relocate his army to the defenses of Vicksburg. The city would now be heavily defended, and any attempt to capture it would require a great commitment in manpower and blood.

In the meantime, Sherman lost his independent command to Maj. Gen. John McClernand, a politically appointed officer with strong ties to the Lincoln administration. McClernand was a Democratic Congressman from southern Illinois who supported the cause of the Union. As such, he had a great amount of influence with like-minded Democratic constituents in the Northwest. McClernand resigned his seat in Congress at the outbreak of the war and raised a full brigade of volunteers for the Union cause. Lincoln, wishing to maintain as wide a base as possible for the war effort, had McClernand commissioned a brigadier general. In March 1862, he was promoted to major general for his participation in the campaign against Fort Donelson. McClernand aspired to command of a field army and began political maneuvering that would hopefully lead to such a command. He came up with a plan he was sure Washington would accept. McClernand proposed to raise a reserve army in the Northwest for the purpose of capturing Vicksburg. He was able to persuade Lincoln to support his plan, and on October 21, 1862, Secretary Stanton granted him authority to raise troops in Indiana, Illinois, and Iowa. Under the terms of his initial orders, McClernand was to report only to General Halleck and would not be under the control of Grant or any other field commander. Halleck was opposed to this arrangement, and by December, he had succeeded in limiting McClernand's authority to the command of one of the two corps he was creating in his new army, under Grant's authority. Sherman was to have command of the other corps. McClernand, being senior in rank to Sherman, would have overall command of both corps when they operated together. Grant ordered Sherman to make his attempt against Vicksburg largely because of this command controversy.

Grant was hoping to decide the issue at Vicksburg before McClernand could take command of his newly raised army. McClernand was still recruiting men when Sherman left Memphis, and he did not arrive in that city until eight days after Sherman's departure. By the time McClernand caught up to Sherman the action at Chickasaw Bluffs had already been fought. On January 4, 1863, Cump relinquished command of the two corps to McClernand and assumed command of the newly designated XV Corps, consisting of two divisions, commanded by Brig. Gens. Frederick Steele and David Stuart.

Once McClernand was on the scene, it soon became apparent to Cump that he had no definite plan of operation against Vicksburg. Sherman said that he "spoke in general terms of opening the navigation of the Mississippi, 'cutting his way to the sea,' etc., etc., but the *modus operandi* was not so clear." Sherman suggested that the Confederate force at Arkansas Post be dealt with before any further operations were undertaken. The Confederates had constructed a large, earthwork fortification, called Fort Hindman, near Arkansas Post, for the purpose of defending the mouth of the Arkansas River and preventing any Union incursions toward Little Rock. The place also served as a base of operations for Confederate Naval vessels to raid Union shipping along the Mississippi. Fort Hindman was an imposing structure, built on a bluff 25 feet above the Arkansas River, and was garrisoned by approximately 5,000 troops, under the command of Brig. Gen. Thomas J. Churchill. The fort's armament faced the river, however, and Sherman felt it would easily fall if attacked from the rear. Sherman convinced McClernand to seek cooperation from Admiral Porter's gunboats in the undertaking, and on January 4, the same day McClernand had arrived to assume command, the pair went in search of Porter, finding him aboard his flagship, the *Black Hawk*.

Porter was hesitant to support the plan, based largely on his personal dislike for McClernand. Cump "begged him, for the sake of harmony, to waive that, which he promised to do." Porter explained to the two officers that he was short on coal for his iron-clad gunboats, and Sherman offered to tow the warships to their destination to save Porter's supply. At length, Porter agreed to lend support to the enterprise. He even decided to lead the Naval expedition in person. Sherman and McClernand made their way back to Milliken's Bend, and the operation was gotten underway at once. The troops transports convoyed by three iron-clad gunboats, sailed down the Mississippi to the White River, which was reached on January 8. They then sailed up the White River to a place known as the cutoff, through which entrance to the Arkansas River could be obtained. By January 9, the expeditionary force had arrived near Fort Hindman, and McClernand began putting his troops ashore that evening. On the morning of January 10, Sherman, at the head of Steele's division, advanced toward the rear of Fort Hindman, capturing the Confederate's first line of defenses. The defenders fell back to positions in and around the fort. That night, Cump decided to reconnoiter the enemy position. "Personally I crept up to a stump so close that I could hear the enemy hard at work, pulling down houses, cutting with axes, and building entrenchments. I could almost hear their words, and was thus listening when, about 4 a.m. the bugler in the rebel camp sounded as pretty a reveille as I ever listened to."

Porter's gunboats pounded Fort Hindman's batteries throughout the day on January 10 and withdrew only with the coming of darkness. On January 11, the Union infantry advanced its field batteries within shelling distance of the fort and added their fire to the renewed bombardment of Porter's ships. All of the cannon in Fort Hindman were silenced by the combined barrage. Porter's gunboats sailed past the fort to take up position to cut off any potential Confederate retreat, and McClernand positioned his men for an attack on the defenses. By this time, it was approximately 4:00 P.M., and McClernand was anxious to launch his assault before darkness cast its pall over the landscape. The Union troops were ordered forward, and for the next half hour a fierce firefight erupted all along the line. At about 4:30 P.M., Sherman noticed "a man jumped up on the rebel parapet just where the road entered, waving a large white flag, and numerous other white rags appeared above the parapet along the whole line. I immediately ordered 'Cease firing!'; and sent the same word down the line to General Steele . . . I ordered my aide, Colonel Dayton, to jump on his horse and ride straight up to the large white flag, and when his horse was on the parapet I followed with the rest of my staff. . . . On entering the line, I saw that our muskets and guns had done good execution; for there was a horse-battery, and every horse lay dead in the traces. The fresh-made parapet had been knocked down in many places, and dead men lay around very thick.

I inquired who commanded at that point, and a Colonel (Robert) Garland stepped up and said that he commanded that brigade. I ordered him to form his brigade, stack arms, hang the belts on the muskets, and stand waiting for orders."

Colonel Garland had been premature in surrendering and had done so without the permission of General Churchill, who intended to fight on. Garland's capitulation compromised the entire Confederate position, however, and made it impossible for Churchill to offer further resistance. Admiral Porter, seeing white flags flying above the fort, led a landing party of sailors to take possession of the works. When Cump entered the works, he found General Churchill conversing with Porter and Brig. Gen. Andrew J. Smith. When Sherman joined the trio, one of his staff officers came to report a situation developing along the Confederate works, in front of General Steele's division. Brig. Gen. James Deshler commanded the Confederate brigade in front of Steele, and he refused to surrender his command on the grounds that he had received no orders from Churchill. Sherman "advised General Churchill to send orders at once, because a single shot might bring the whole of Steele's division on Deshler's brigade, and I would not be responsible for the consequences; soon afterward, we both concluded to go in person." Upon reaching Deshler's position, Churchill issued orders for the surrender of the brigade, and the capture of Fort Hindman was complete. Union losses in the campaign totaled 1,061 in killed, wounded, and missing, while the Confederates sustained casualties of nearly 5,500, with almost 4,800 of those being captured.

General Grant was furious over the expedition to Arkansas Post and blamed McClernand for straying from his overall strategy to capture Vicksburg. Grant did not realize that Sherman had been the architect of the campaign, and McClernand was only following his advice, and held McClernand completely responsible for what he felt to be an ill-advised lark. Upon learning the truth, that the expedition had been Cump's idea, Grant quickly changed his tune and began praising the mission for accomplishing great good for the Union cause. McClernand was ordered to bring his army back to Mississippi. By the end of January, Grant arrived in person and concentrated his command. He would have approximately 45,000 men, divided into three corps, under the command of Sherman, McClernand, and James McPherson.

Admiral Porter's Western Flotilla would provide naval support with his 11 gunboats and various other vessels.

Grant was upset with McClernand because of the political intrigue he had used in attempting to gain an independent command, and the charge that he had compromised the campaign against Vicksburg was merely a cover. The fact was it was almost impossible to mount a campaign against Vicksburg during the winter, as that was the rainy season, and most of the approaches to the city were flooded and impassable. Vicksburg occupied an almost impregnable position, situated on high bluffs, at a horseshoe bend of the Mississippi River. The land on either side of the bluffs, nearest to the river, was known as the Delta, and was a strip of swampy, densely vegetated land, bisected by rivers and swamps that was almost impassable to an invading army. The land across the river from Vicksburg, in Louisiana, was exactly the same as the Delta and presented the same problems. In order to mount a campaign against the city, it would be necessary for Grant to place his army on high ground and get to the ridgeline that the city occupied, but getting there was the problem. The north and west sides of the city were protected by the swamps and Delta. To move his army to the south of the city, Grant would have to run his transports and Porter's gunboats through a gauntlet of artillery fire from Vicksburg's guns for a great many miles, while the ships tried to navigate the terrific bend in the river. There was simply no good option, and it seemed as if the topographical strength of the position made it foolhardy to even attempt an assault against it. But Grant was determined to try every available means of getting at Vicksburg. He put his men to digging and constructed three different canals intended to give his ships a way in which to bypass the horseshoe bend in the Mississippi and allow them to enter the river south of the city. All of the canal efforts proved to be failures, but Grant reasoned he was keeping his men occupied and focused while he cast about for other options.

Another avenue of approach that was explored was the various rivers and streams that cut through the Delta all around Vicksburg. If one of them could be found that was capable of navigation by his transports and gunboats, he could place his army on dry ground to the north or east of the city. Several expeditions were undertaken in search of a water route around Vicksburg's flank. Ships were sent up the Yazoo

River and Steele's bayou in search of a way to get behind the Confederate position, but each expedition ended in failure.

By April 1863, Grant was no closer to Vicksburg than he had been
in December, and a public outcry began against what most people felt
to be bungling efforts on his part. President Lincoln stood firm in his
support of him, however. Lincoln said, "I don't know what to make of
Grant, he's such a quiet little fellow. The only way I know he's around
is by the way he makes things go." When pressed to remove Grant from
command, Lincoln responded, "I think we'll try him a little longer."

April sunshine proved to be just what Grant had been waiting for.
With the rainy season over, roads began to dry out, and conditions
vastly improved for offensive operations. Grant proposed to march a
portion of his army down the Louisiana side of the river, to a point
south of Vicksburg. He would then transport them across the Mississippi and lay siege to the city from its rear. On March 29, Grant ordered
McClernand's corps to cut a road through the Louisiana swampland
from Milliken's Bend to a point south of Vicksburg. The work was completed in short order, and by April 16, Grant was ready to put his plan
in motion. Porter's flotilla was to run past the Vicksburg batteries that
night. Confederate pickets, stationed in boats on the river, spotted the
vessels and gave the alarm. Tar barrels along the bank were lighted,
and houses on the opposite shore were set ablaze to illuminate the river
and make the Union ships clearly visible to Confederate gunners. As
the first of the Federals ships steamed into range, the big guns of Vicksburg opened fire. Porter's gunboats responded, and in the night air was
shaken by the blasts of the opposing cannon. Each ship steamed slowly
past several miles of enemy gun emplacements. Every one of Porter's
vessels sustained numerous hits from the Confederate guns, and several
were put out of commission. Only one of the ships was sunk, however,
and the rest made it to the village of Hard Times, 25 miles south of
Vicksburg, where they found Grant and his infantry waiting. In a few
days, Porter had repaired the damage done to the ships by the bombardment and was ready once more to assist Grant in the next phase of his
campaign.

Grant's intention was to operate from south of the city, but he
wanted to keep Pemberton guessing about his plans. Accordingly, he
initiated two operations on April 17 designed to keep the Confederate

commander off-balance. Col. Benjamin Grierson departed from Tennessee on that day with 1,000 Union cavalrymen, on one of the most celebrated raids of the war. Grierson and his troopers marched through the state of Mississippi, to the east of Vicksburg, destroying all Confederate supplies and lines of communication they could before eventually making their way to Baton Rouge. Sherman, who had not yet departed from Milliken's Bend, was to launch a diversionary assault to the north of Vickburg. Cump's orders were to send a division against Haines's Bluff to convince Pemberton that Grant's main assault would be coming from that direction. Maj. Gen. Francis P. Blair Jr. was ordered to make the feint with his division, supported by naval gunboats. Grant was hesitant to place Sherman in command of this mission, however. As Cump explained it, "he did not like to order me to do it, because it might be reported at the North that I had again been 'repulsed, etc.' . . . Of course I answered him that I would make the 'feint,' regardless of public clamor at a distance, and I did make it most effectively." Sherman pulled off the feint perfectly. Blair's troops demonstrated against the Confederate defenses in a most convincing manner, and the Union gunboats shelled the Southern works in what appeared to be a bombardment preparatory to a general assault. General Pemberton had previously dispatched a large body of troops to reinforce Brig. Gen. John S. Bowen's brigade, at Grand Gulf, where Grant was expected to attack. Cump's diversion caused Pemberton to recall those reinforcements and send them to Haines's Bluff, to oppose Blair's men. Grant would therefore be facing a greatly reduced enemy when he made his crossing and positioned his army on the Mississippi side of the river.

Once Sherman's assignment was completed, Blair's troops were removed from Haines's Bluff and returned to Milliken's Bend. The feint could not have been accomplished better, and the fact that casualties to the Union forces amounted to only one man wounded made it even more spectacular. Cump then started his corps on the march to join Grant and the main body, following the 70-mile-path through the Delta on the Louisiana shore that their comrades had already taken. By May 6, Sherman's men had reached Hard Times, and Grant's army was reunited. Grant was already across the river. On April 30, McClernand's corps was landed on the Mississippi shore, at Bruinsburg, and pushed forward to occupy a line of bluffs 3 miles inland. Gen. John

Bowen, with 8,000 Confederate troops, moved from Grand Gulf to oppose the Federal advance, at Port Gibson, 30 miles south of Vicksburg.
On May 1, Bowen's command formed a line of battle just outside of Port
Gibson and prepared to contest McClernand's advance. The Confederates were outnumbered by almost three-to-one, but were aided materially by the rugged terrain of the area that prevented McClernand from
bringing his whole force to bear against the defenders. Fighting lasted
throughout the day, as Bowen slowly gave ground. By the time darkness brought a close to the battle, the Confederates had been forced
through the town of Port Gibson and had withdrawn from the field.
Casualties were approximately 800 on both sides. Although not a large
battle, the outcome of the engagement at Port Gibson was crucial to
Grant's plans, as it gave him control of the three roads leading out of
the town, to Grand Gulf, Vicksburg, and Jackson.

Sherman's corps crossed over from Louisiana and joined Grant's
main body on May 7. Grant had received intelligence that a large force
of Confederates were being gathered together at Jackson, 45 miles
east of Vicksburg, under the command of Gen. Joseph E. Johnston.
Grant decided to march directly between the forces of Pemberton and
Johnston and to defeat them separately before their forces could be
combined against him. This would necessitate severing his line of supplies from Porter's flotilla and subsisting his army on the enemy countryside. It would also mean that he was placing his force between two
enemy armies that outnumbered his and could operate to cut off and
destroy his army. The plan was audacious and would rely on speed of
movement to pull it off, but Grant was confident of success. Cump
protested against the plan, and as Grant remembered it, told him "that
I was putting myself in a position voluntarily which an enemy would
be glad to maneuver a year—or a long time—to get me." Grant threw
caution to the wind, however, and put his plan into motion the same
day Sherman's corps arrived. McClernand's corps was left behind to
guard against Pemberton, while Grant pointed his other two corps
toward Jackson. McPherson's corps was on the left, marching along
the Clinton Road, while Sherman, on the right, used a road passing
through Mississippi Springs. On May 12, McPherson's corps fought a
small battle against a Confederate force led by Brig. Gen. John Gregg
at Raymond. McPherson had a three-to-one superiority in men and a

seven-to-one edge in artillery. McPherson routed Gregg from the field, but not before engaging in a sharp struggle that cost 446 Union casualties and 820 Confederate losses. The fighting at Raymond did not hamper McPherson's march. He and Sherman both arrived at Jackson on May 14.

Gen. Joseph E. Johnston had been gathering together an army at Jackson, but by the time Grant arrived at the outskirts of the city he had only been able to concentrate 12,000 men. Grant's two corps had more than twice that and after offering a brief resistance outside of town, Johnston determined to abandon Jackson and retreat to the north. The brigades of General Gregg and Brig. Gen. William H. T. Walker were posted as a rearguard to allow Johnston time to remove valuable military stores from the city. Grant delayed his attack, because of a driving rainstorm that would have ruined the black powder in the soldier's cartridges, but when the downpour slackened, he sent his regiments forward in a resistless wave that swept the rearguard from the field. Cump reported that they had captured "three entire field batteries, and about two hundred prisoners of war."

Grant did not pursue Johnston's forces. Instead, he directed his attention toward Vicksburg. On the morning of May 15, McPherson's corps began marching toward Edward's Station and a rendezvous with McClernand's corps. Sherman was ordered to remain in Jackson to destroy the military stores in the city, along with an arsenal, a foundry, and cotton mill, and as much railroad track as he could. Cump's men went to work with a vengeance, but by the morning of May 16, Grant sent word that a battle near Edward's Station was eminent and requested Cump to send one of his divisions. Steele's division was ordered to Grant's support, and Sherman followed with the remainder of his force later that day. A battle was indeed in the making. Pemberton had sallied forth from Vicksburg with 22,000 men to attack the Union supply line from Grand Gulf to Raymond. He was in the process of this when Grant's vanguard made contact with Pemberton's army at 7:00 A.M., and the Confederates quickly formed a three-mile defensive line along the crest of Champion Hill. Grant arrived at 10:00 A.M. and ordered McClernand and McPherson to attack. The battle raged for three hours, until 1:00 P.M., when Union forces penetrated the center of the Confederate line and seized the crest of the hill. The

Confederates charged and drove the Federals off the crest, but did not have the manpower to sustain the attack. General Pemberton ordered the division of Maj. Gen. William W. Loring, on the right, to march to the support of the embattled troops in the center. Loring pulled his men out of line and began a circuitous route to the Confederate center. In the meantime, Grant launched a counterattack, using fresh troops that had just arrived on the field, and the Confederate center was broken. Pemberton had little choice but to abandon the field and retreat over the one escape route still left open to him: the Raymond Road. General Loring's division now found itself cut off from the rest of Pemberton's command and was forced to make a three-day march around Grant's forces to join Johnston. Grant's army suffered 2,457 losses in the battle of Champion Hill, while inflicting 3,840 casualties on the Confederate forces. In addition, Pemberton was deprived the services of General Loring's entire division for the remainder of the campaign.

Sherman missed the fight at Champion Hill, but Grant intended to give him a key role following that engagement. Grant planned to push ahead with the corps of McClernand and McPherson, while Cump made a march to the right, crossing the Big Black at a point north of Pemberton's defensive position. Grant hoped to pin the enemy down long enough for Sherman to gain their rear and cut them off from Vicksburg. Caught out in the open, Pemberton's army would be trapped between superior forces, and Grant hoped to it.

Pemberton placed his army behind hastily constructed works, with their backs to the Big Black River. He hoped to guard the bridges until General Loring could join him, still unaware that Loring and his men were heading in the opposite direction. Early on the morning of May 17, Grant's forces made contact with Pemberton, and Union artillery opened with a barrage. Brig. Gen. Eugene Carr's division charged the Confederate works, without orders, causing panic among the Southern troops. Fearing that they would be cut off, many defenders ran for the bridges to make good their escape. Pemberton's line was crumbling, so he ordered a withdrawal. The bridges were burned after his troops had crossed, as his army hurried toward Vicksburg. Grant's army captured 1,000 prisoners and 18 cannon, but Pemberton had slipped the trap and was in full flight toward his strong defenses. Sherman had been unable to interpose his forces between Pemberton's army and

Vicksburg owing to the precipitous retreat the Confederates had made from the Big Black, but he moved his corps toward the city to the north of Grant.

Once Grant's forces were assembled before Vicksburg, they were positioned around the city. Sherman's corps formed the right of the Union line, with Cump's right flank at Haines's Bluff, where contact was made with the Federal fleet. General McPherson's corps formed the center of Grant's line and was extended to the left by McClernand's corp. The Union position was governed by the Confederate defenses and formed a semicircle around Vicksburg.

Pemberton used the time since being appointed commander of the Department of Mississippi and West Louisiana to greatly improve the defenses of Vicksburg. He oversaw the construction of a nine-mile arc of works that screened the rear of the city from its start, at the Mississippi River, north of the city, to its termination at the shoreline south of Vicksburg. The geography of the area was one of bluffs, separated by deeply cut ravines. Along the crest of six ridges of high ground that radiated out of the city had been laid the roads to other parts of Mississippi. These roadways offered a precarious route into and out of the city, as the ground on either side dropped off into deep gullies and ravines. Pemberton had constructed forts at key points along his line. There were nine, with six of these being built to command the roads leading to the city. The forts were earthwork structures, having walls up to 20-feet thickness. In front of each fort a deep, a wide ditch had been dug to increase the difficulty for an enemy force attempting to assault the works. The forts were connected by a line of rifle pits with parapets and ditches of their own. Pemberton had placed 128 pieces of artillery in these works, 36 of which were heavy siege guns. All in all, it was a formidable position, boasting the strongest defensive works to be found in the country. In later years, after visiting the famed works at Sevastopol, Cump would proclaim that the fortifications at Vicksburg were stronger by far.

General Grant had become convinced that the recent defeats at Champion's Hill and the Big Black River had demoralized Pemberton's men and felt that an all out attack could seize the city. Accordingly, he issued orders to his corps commanders to make an assault on the enemy works on May 19. Sherman's corps was already in position to make such an attack. Grant's other two corps had just reached the city and were less prepared for the assault. At 2:00 P.M., the attack went forward. Sherman's troops charged amidst a hail of enemy fire, making a temporary lodgment near the walls of Stockade Redan before being repulsed. Cump stated that his "troops reached the top of the parapet, but could not cross over. The rebel parapets were strongly manned, and the enemy fought hard and well. My loss was pretty heavy."

The assaults of Grant's other two corps met with even less success. McPherson and McClernand were able to get no closer than a couple hundred yards to the Confederate works. Union losses came to nearly 1,000 killed and wounded, while the Confederates suffered only 70 casualties. Grant's attempt to capture Vicksburg by storm had been repulsed, but the Federal leader was not yet resigned to laying siege to the city. Grant decided to launch one more full-scale assault against the city on May 22. He would use his 220 cannon, assisted by the big guns of Admiral Porter's fleet, to soften up the enemy works before his troops attacked. Ladders would be provided to the attacking regiments so that they could scale the steep sides of the Confederate forts. Cump looked for a way to bridge the ditch in front of his primary objective, but there were no boards to be found. The only source of such material was the house General Grant made his headquarters. When Sherman explained his need for the lumber, Grant moved out of the residence. Cump's men tore down the structure on May 21.

Grant set the time of the attack for 10:00 A.M., and Sherman's men rushed forward at that precise moment. One hundred and fifty volunteers from his command were out in front of the attacking line. These men carried the boards from Grant's headquarters, in hopes of placing them across the ditch for the following troops. As the Union troops advanced, Cump reported that the Confederates showed "no sign of unusual activity, but as our troops came in fair view, the enemy rose behind their parapets and poured a furious fire upon our lines; and for about two hours, we had a severe and bloody battle, but at every point we were repulsed."

On the left of the Union line, General McClernand had made a brief lodgment in the Railroad Redoubt, when several men from the 22nd Iowa entered the fort through a hole in the wall caused by artillery fire. The stay of the Iowa troops was of short duration, however,

Union troops attacking Confederate defenses at Vicksburg, Mississippi. (U.S. Military History Institute)

when a company of Texas troops counterattacked and drove them out of the works. McClernand was encouraged by this small success and asked for a renewal of the attack, along the entire line, so that he could exploit his gain. Accordingly, Grant ordered Sherman and McPherson to commit their reserves to another assault, to provide a diversion for McClernand's assault. The fact was that McClernand had not breached the Confederate line, and the second assault was shattered with terrible losses. Union losses were 3,199, as opposed to less than 500 casualties inflicted on the Confederates. Grant was convinced that Vicksburg could not be taken by storm and immediately began implementing siege operations to bombard city into submission.

Over the course of the next five weeks, the Union army dug several miles of trenches as it crept ever closer to the Confederate works. Artillery from Grant's field batteries and the heavy guns of Porter's fleet bombarded the city constantly, in an effort to protect the digging efforts and demoralize the defenders. By May 31, Grant had received reinforcements from Memphis and had extended his lines in a 12-mile arc to cut off Vicksburg from the outside world. His main concern now was that Gen. Joseph E. Johnston might decide to attack his rear in an effort to raise the siege and rescue Pemberton's forces. Grant was anxious over Johnston's movements and confided to Sherman that Johnston was the only Confederate commander he feared. Cump was detailed to command troops Grant was gathering in his rear to defend against any attempts Johnston might make on behalf of Pemberton.

Cump was given one division from each of Grant's three corps, plus two divisions of Maj. Gen. John G. Parke's newly arrived corps. Sherman arranged these five divisions in an arc in the rear of Grant's army, stretching from Haines's Bluff to the Big Black River. Scouting parties were sent out to search for signs of Johnston, but the Confederate commander made no effort to cross the Big Black River and assail Sherman. The arrival of Parke's corps had raised the number of men in Grant's army to over 77,000, and Johnston was hesitant to tangle with such a formidable foe. By July 1, the situation in Vicksburg had become critical, and the chance of relieving the garrison before it capitulated had almost disappeared. The soldiers and civilians in the city had been virtually without food for five weeks and had been compelled to eat horses, mules, and even rats. Starved, weakened, and exposed to the relentless bombardment of the Federal siege guns, the inhabitants of Vicksburg had stood as much as they could take. Johnston recognized the hopelessness of the situation and withdrew his command to Jackson. On July 3, Pemberton sent a message through the lines asking Grant for terms of surrender. Grant offered to parole Pemberton's troops after their surrender, making them ineligible to serve in the Southern military until they had been exchanged for a like number of Federal troops. Pemberton agreed, and July 4 was set as the date for the formal surrender of the city. Grant had succeeded in capturing the great Confederate bastion of Vicksburg. The only Confederate stronghold remaining on the Mississippi was now at Port Hudson, and that would be captured shortly by forces under the command of Maj. Gen. Nathaniel Banks. Pemberton's army had been greatly reduced by losses at the battles of Champion's Hill and Big Black River, but the force he surrendered to Grant was still more than 29,000 strong.

With the fall of Vicksburg, Grant was now free to focus his attention on Joe Johnston. Sherman was ordered to march on Jackson to destroy Johnston's army. Cump would be in command of three corps for the operation: his own, General Parke's, and General McClernand's, now under the command of Maj. Gen. Edward O.C. Ord. McClernand had been relieved of command by General Grant for issues arising during the Vicksburg Campaign. Sherman got underway at once, and two corps were across the Big Black by July 6. General Johnston tried to impede Sherman's progress by fouling the water supplies along his line of march. Cows and sheep were taken into ponds along Sherman's line of approach to Jackson and were shot and left to contaminate the water supply. This ploy did little to slow down the Federals, and by July 10, Cump had his army on the outskirts of Jackson. "On the 11th we pressed close in, and shelled the town from every direction. One of Ord's brigades (Lauman's) got too close, and was very roughly handled and driven back in disorder."

The Confederate defenders had constructed strong field works around the city, and Cump, with the memory of the two failed frontal assaults against Vicksburg still fresh in his mind, chose not to throw his men upon them. Instead, he conducted a siege, hoping for the same results as had crowned Union efforts against Pemberton's army. But Johnston was not Pemberton. He had no intention of allowing himself to be trapped in Jackson. The city had little strategic importance, and he was not about to lose his army defending it. On the evening of July 16, Johnston began an evacuation of the city, and by the following morning, Union forces found the place deserted. Cump sent General Steele's division after Johnston, but called off the pursuit after 14 miles, stating "in that hot weather it would have been fatal to my command" to have continued it further. He had failed to capture or destroy Johnston's army, but the Confederates had been driven from the region. On July 8, Port Hudson fell to forces under Nathaniel Banks, and the Union gained complete control of the vital waterway. As President Lincoln put it, the Mississippi now went "unvexed to the sea."

Chapter 11

MAKING GEORGIA HOWL

The capture of Vicksburg was followed by a well-earned period of rest for the men of Grant's army. There was also a disbursement of the forces under Grant's command. General Ord's corps was sent down the Mississippi and thence to Texas. General Parke's corps was returned to Kentucky. This left Grant with three corps: McPherson's, at Vicksburg; Steven Hurlburt's, at Memphis; and Sherman's, 20 miles east of Vicksburg. With the promise of an extended lull in the action, Ellen brought their four children to visit Cump in camp. Willie was nine years old, and, like most boys, deeply interested in all things military. He quickly became a favorite in camp and was often seen riding along with his father on inspections of the camps. Cump took the family on frequent visits to Vicksburg, where Ellen and the children had the opportunity to visit Grant's wife and children. Sherman enjoyed the company of his family and certainly welcomed this period of rest, but his active mind could not help but think that the Union was missing an opportunity to deal a death blow to the Confederacy. Sherman did not believe that Grant's army should be split up. He felt that the administration was missing a golden opportunity by not allowing his superior to continue his offensive operations against the enemy.

As the summer progressed, events remained quiet in Mississippi and Virginia. The only Union army actively campaigning was Maj. Gen. William S. Rosecrans's Army of the Cumberland. On June 24, Rosecrans had undertaken the Tullahoma Campaign to drive Gen. Braxton Bragg's Army of Tennessee out of the middle portion of the state for which it was named. Chattanooga, Tennessee was Rosecrans's ultimate goal. The city was of great strategic importance as a transportation hub and as the guardian of the Confederacy's heartland. Through a series of brilliant maneuvers, Rosecrans was able to force Bragg through Tennessee, and on September 9, Chattanooga fell to the Army of the Cumberland without a fight. Rosecrans, thinking that Bragg was retreating with his army to Atlanta, divided his force and pursued through the mountains of northwestern Georgia. But Bragg was not retreating. He had been reinforced by Lt. Gen. James P. Longstreet's corps, of the Army of Northern Virginia, and was waiting to attack Rosecrans's segmented forces. On September 19, the Confederates attacked in the two-day battle of Chickamauga. Rosecrans's army suffered a bloody defeat and was forced to retreat back to Chattanooga, where it was besieged by the Army of Tennessee. The two great Union victories of the year now seemed to be in jeopardy. An entire Union army was trapped in Chattanooga and in danger of being captured. The Confederates had indeed regained the initiative, as Cump had feared, and threatened to negate all of the accomplishments that had been gained by Union arms. In the North, the Lincoln administration looked for a leader to bring order out of the chaos in southeastern Tennessee. Grant was felt to be the man for the job. Accordingly, he was given overall command of the Union armies in the Western Theater, except those in Louisiana, and directed to proceed to Chattanooga to supervise operations to relieve the siege of that city. Sherman was left in command of the Army of the Tennessee, with orders to march a large contingent of that army toward Chattanooga. Cump marched his command, consisting of his own 15th Corps, and a division of the 17th Corps, to Memphis, and then turned east toward Chattanooga.

On the boat trip from Vicksburg to Memphis, nine-year-old Willie became ill with typhoid fever. By the time the Shermans reached Memphis, on October 2, the boy was gravely ill and clinging to life. Willie died on October 3. Sherman was stunned. "The blow was a terrible one to us all," he wrote, "so sudden and so unexpected, that I could not help reproaching myself for having consented to his visit in that sickly region in the summer-time." The family procured a small casket for the boy, and Mrs. Sherman, along with the rest of the children, took the body back to St. Louis for burial. A heartbroken Sherman turned his thoughts to his responsibilities and the mission at hand. "On, on I must go," he wrote, "to meet a soldier's fate, or live to see our country rise superior to all the factions, till the flag is adored and respected by ourselves and by all the powers of the earth." He had witnessed death that tore families asunder many times on the battlefield, but this was the first time that the cost of the war was brought home to his very doorstep.

There was little time for the grieving father to mourn the death of his son. Other sons were in peril, in Chattanooga, and swift action was required to save them from their predicament. Sherman boarded a train at Memphis, and on October 11, reached Collierville, Tennessee. The town was under attack from Confederate cavalry when Cump arrived, and the 800 Union defenders were being sorely pressed by the Confederate troopers, numbering more than 2,500 strong. Sherman took command of the Union defenses and successfully repulsed the Southern efforts to seize the town.

Cump's orders were to repair the tracks of the Memphis and Charleston Railroad along his line of march. Rosecrans's army, in Chattanooga, was desperately short of supplies, and the rail lines would be needed to support his beleaguered forces. Once Sherman's relief force reached Athens, Alabama, he was to make contact with Rosecrans to receive further instructions. On October 21, Grant met with General Rosecrans and Maj. Gen. Joseph Hooker at Nashville, Tennessee, to discuss operations around Chattanooga. The War Department had ordered the XI and XII Corps of the Army of the Potomac, under the command of General Hooker, to proceed to Chattanooga with all haste to reinforce Rosecrans's army. Some 23,000 veterans of the Eastern campaigns were transported by rail to Stephenson, Alabama, a distance of almost 1,200 miles, in the course of a week. Grant reached Chattanooga on October 23. The first item of importance was to open a line of supply for the besieged garrison. Gen. George Henry Thomas and Brig. Gen. William F. Smith had previously devised a plan to reopen communications with Bridgeport, Alabama through Lookout Valley, by means of capturing Brown's Ferry, on the opposite shore of the Tennessee River. In the early morning hours of October 27, a force of approximately 1,200 men, commanded by Brig. Gen. William B. Hazen, floated down the Tennessee River on pontoon boats, landing at Brown's Ferry, at 5:00 A.M. Hazen's men drove away the Confederate pickets and immediately began to dig entrenchments and establish a beachhead. Brig. Gen. John B. Turchin marched his brigade to Moccasin Point, opposite Brown's Ferry, and when Hazen's troops had established themselves on the Confederate shoreline, he began ferrying his brigade across the river on rowboats. By 10:00 A.M., the Union forces were firmly entrenched at Brown's Ferry, and a pontoon bridge across the river had been completed. General Hooker advanced a portion of his command, from Bridgeport, Alabama, to make contact with the men at the ferry. The successful operation opened a line of supplies the soldiers called the "Cracker Line" between Bridgeport and Chattanooga. The garrison was no longer in danger of being starved into submission.

Braxton Bragg was aware of the concentration of Federal troops in and around Chattanooga. Hooker's two corps were already on the scene, and Sherman's reinforcements from the Army of Tennessee were on their way. In addition, Maj. Gen. Ambrose E. Burnside was in Knoxville, commanding the Union IX Corps. Bragg knew that if the various Union armies were allowed to combine against him, his own army would be vastly outnumbered and in danger of capture or destruction. Accordingly, he devised a plan to defeat the Union armies in detail, before any concentration could be effected. Bragg's plan was to send Lt. Gen. James P. Longstreet's corps to Knoxville to destroy Burnside's force. Bragg hoped that this move would eliminate one of the several Union detachments arrayed against him. He further hoped that Grant would be compelled to send forces from in and around Chattanooga to Burnside's relief, further weakening the enemy army facing him. The plan failed to accomplish either objective. Grant saw the removal of Longstreet's corps as an opportunity for offensive action and sent word to Sherman to stop all work on the railroad and hasten to Chattanooga with all possible speed.

Sherman pushed his command forward, reaching Bridgeport on November 14. The following day, Cump joined Grant in Chattanooga, and the two surveyed the enemy positions on the heights around the town and discussed plans for the coming assault. Sherman's men were to form the left of Grant's line. General Thomas's Army of the Cumberland was to hold the center. Joe Hooker's troops would be on the right. Grant planned to feint with Hooker's troops, against Lookout Mountain and the Confederate left, on the southern portion of Missionary Ridge. His main assault would be commanded by Sherman, against the northern portion of Missionary Ridge, in the vicinity of Tunnel Hill. In order to confuse the Confederates, and keep Bragg guessing, Thomas's forces would be advanced in the center to capture Orchard Knob, a knoll situated between the Union lines and the base of Missionary Ridge. The date set for the assault was November 21, but that had to be postponed due to difficulty in getting Sherman's men into position.

On October 23, elements of the Army of the Cumberland advanced and seized Orchard Knob. The following day, Hooker's forces advanced to assault the left flank of the Confederate line. The day was exceptionally foggy, and as Hooker's men engaged Confederates on Lookout Mountain, the progress of the battle could only be followed by means of the soldiers' musket flashes. Hooker's troops were fiercely engaged by the Confederates on Lookout Mountain, but by the end of the day, they had managed to drive the defenders from many of their lower defensive positions. General Bragg ordered its evacuation that night, and when the sun rose on the morning of October 25, the national colors were seen flying from the crest. Thus far, Hooker's part in the campaign had been a great success. General Thomas had suggested to Grant that the Confederate left was the proper place to mount his main effort to turn the enemy flank, and had advised that Hooker's force take the leading role in the battle. Grant, however, chose the Confederate right as his main objective, where Sherman would be entrusted with the job of dislodging the enemy from his prepared works.

By October 25, Sherman had his divisions in position and was ready for the general assault. Hooker's forces engaged Bragg's left, on the southern tip of Missionary Ridge, while Sherman assaulted the northern end of the ridge near Tunnel Hill. Thomas was to keep the Army of the Cumberland in readiness to assault the center of Missionary Ridge as soon as Cump was able to turn the Confederate right flank.

Sherman's attacks began at about 10:00 A.M., when he sent six divisions, totaling 26,000 men, forward against the Confederate line. The Confederates had two divisions opposed to Sherman, under Maj. Gens. Patrick Cleburne and Carter Stevenson. These two divisions totaled only 10,000 men, giving Sherman more than a two-to-one advantage. But the Confederates occupied a strong defensive line and were fighting from behind earthworks. The strength of the position more than compensated for the defenders lack of numbers. When Sherman's lines surged forward toward the enemy position they were greeted with a murderous hail of artillery and musket fire that blunted the assault and sent it hurling backward. Sherman's men reformed and charged again, several times, but each renewed assault met with the same results. In several instances, the Confederates would leave their works to counterattack the retreating Federals. Bayonets and clubbed muskets were used freely in these hand-to-hand melees, as each side fought with dogged determination. Sherman's casualties were mounting, with no success being achieved. Approximately 2,000 Union soldiers fell in the various assaults against the Confederate position. Sherman would later make an unbecoming accusation when he asserted that his assaults had failed because they were not supported by General Thomas's army. Thomas was ordered to attack only after the Confederate flank had been turned, and this Sherman failed to do.

In the meantime, General Hooker located the left flank of Bragg's army. By 3:00 P.M., his troops had started to pry the brigade of Brig. Gen. Henry D. Clayton out of their works. Hooker's troops gained the crest of the ridge and captured hundreds of Confederate prisoners. Grant and Thomas observed the movement of Hooker's troops from Orchard Knob, and when it appeared that the Confederate left was beginning to give way, Grant ordered Thomas to send the Army of the Cumberland forward to capture the rifle pits at the base of Missionary Ridge. Maj. Gen. Gordon Granger was to lead assault, amounting to 20,000 men. The Union troops surged forward at a fast pace, and as they neared the first line of Confederate rifle pits they were met by a volley from the enemy. Undaunted, Granger's men closed the gaps and drove on. In a matter of minutes, they overran the rifle pits, capturing hundreds of prisoners. But Thomas's men now found themselves in a precarious situation. The Confederates had constructed several lines of defense along the face of the mountain, and the Union troops were now exposed to the plunging fire from the defenders above. To remain where they were would have been suicide, as every volley from the slope cut down scores of Union troops. To retreat would have forced the troops to recross the open ground they had just charged over, easy targets for enemy infantry and artillery massed on the ridge. The men in the ranks seemed to grasp the realities of the situation at once. Individually and in small groups, men started ascending the slope to attack the Confederates raining death down upon them. In a matter of seconds, companies and regiments started to sweep up the side of the mountain, until Granger's entire command had joined in the assault. In one of the grandest charges made by either side during the war, the Army of the Cumberland charged, without orders, against what had been thought to be the impregnable defenses on Missionary Ridge. The impetuousness of their charge became a resistless wave, as they refused to be denied. The blue lines swept up the hill until their regimental banners could be seen floating in the breeze on the crest. Bragg's army had been broken, and as the defenders of Missionary Ridge ran for the rear, Bragg ordered a retreat from the field. The battles for Chattanooga proved to be a tremendous victory for the Union, and Grant received the lion's share of the credit. His star was in its ascendancy, and Grant's rise would cause Sherman to come to the forefront of leadership in the war.

Following the victory at Missionary Ridge, Grant turned his attention to the relief of Burnside's forces at Knoxville. General Longstreet had laid siege to the city and was threatening to starve Burnside's 12,000 troops into submission. Sherman was ordered to lead a relief column of 20,000 men to drive Longstreet away from Knoxville and lift the siege. Sherman's troops plodded through bitter winter conditions for 83 miles to reach Knoxville. Rations were in short supply, many of his troops were without blankets, and some were barefoot, but the command pushed forward without complaint. On November 29, General Longstreet launched an attack against Knoxville's defenses, hoping to carry the city before help could arrive from Chattanooga. Approximately 4,000 troops were thrown against Burnside's works, but were repulsed with heavy casualties. Longstreet's command lost about 800 men in this assault, as opposed to only 20 casualties suffered by the defenders. At the time of Longstreet's assault, the Federal relief column was still some distance from Knoxville. Cump sent his cavalry ahead, and on December 3, the Union troopers reached Burnside. On December 5, Sherman received word from Burnside that Longstreet had withdrawn his forces. His own failed assault, combined with the advance of Sherman's troops, made staying at Knoxville, a risk he was not willing to take. Longstreet's force marched to the northeastern tip of Tennessee, where it spent the winter of 1863–64. In the spring of 1864 Longstreet would cross into Virginia and rejoin Robert E. Lee's Army of Northern Virginia in time for the Wilderness Campaign.

Chattanooga, the key to the Confederate heartland of Georgia, was now safely in Union hands. Knoxville was secure and Southern forces had finally been cleared from East Tennessee. The Chattanooga Campaign had been a huge success, and the war in the West was going in favor of the Union. For his part in the campaign, Cump was officially tendered the thanks of Congress on February 19, 1864. Indeed, events had gone so successfully for the western armies that the Lincoln administration began to look to the West for a solution to bring the war to a conclusion. Grant's star was in its ascendancy, and he was acclaimed as the hero of the nation and the country's top soldier. Congressman Elihu Washburne introduced a bill in the House of Representatives to reinstate the rank of lieutenant general in the U.S. army, for the purpose of conferring that grade to Grant. George Washington had been the only American officer to previously hold the rank, and in honor to Washington, it had never been bestowed upon another general. To be sure, Winfield Scott had been promoted to lieutenant general, but it was only a brevet, and not permanent, grade. The promotion would mean that Grant would be in command of all the Union armies, and while few congressmen had reservations about giving him top command, there was considerable debate over reviving the rank and putting him on the same lofty plain with Washington. In the end, the bill received enough votes, and on March 3, Grant was called East, to Washington, to receive his promotion from President Lincoln. He arrived in the capital on March 8, and the following day received his commission.

Grant determined to remain in the East and accompany Maj. Gen. George G. Meade's Army of the Potomac in its spring campaign against

Robert E. Lee's Army of Northern Virginia. After meeting with Meade, he left Washington on March 11 for Nashville, to discuss his overall strategy with Sherman. Cump was to take Grant's place as commander of the Western Theater, and James McPherson was promoted to assume command of the Army of the Tennessee. Grant's plan was a simple one. The war, to date, had been fought in a series of uncoordinated battles by the various Union armies, allowing the Confederates to make the best use of their interior lines to shift forces back and forth to meet the enemy in threatened areas. What Grant proposed was a concerted effort of all Union armies to deprive the enemy from using their interior lines and bring the full weight of the North's superior numbers to bear. It would be a war of attrition, a war the Confederates could not hope to win. Grant knew that fighting in such a way would produce extreme casualties, but he reasoned that the losses would be no higher than they would if the war was allowed to continue for an extended period.

Part of Grant's strategy involved making Confederate armies, not Southern cities, his prime military objective. For his part, he would use the Army of the Potomac to grab on to Lee's Army of Northern Virginia, and would press, push, and battle the enemy until he had worn Lee's army down to the point that it was no longer an effective military force. Sherman was instructed to march his forces toward Atlanta, and do the same to Gen. Joseph E. Johnston's Army of Tennessee. While all this was going on, Maj. Gen. Franz Sigel was to march an army into the Shenandoah Valley and defeat any enemy found there. Maj. Gen. Benjamin Butler was to lead the Army of the James against Richmond and Petersburg, and Maj. Gen. George Crook was to operate against the Virginia & Tennessee Railroad from his position in West Virginia. The Confederates would be assailed from all sides and could not possibly contend with the pressure. At some point, their defenses must crack, and Grant would then exploit the weakness. All commands were ordered to commence their portion of the offensive as soon as roads in their region were dry enough to allow active campaigning.

Sherman approved of Grant's strategy. "That we are now all to act upon a common plan, converging on a common centre, looks like enlightened War," he wrote to his superior. "Like yourself, you take the biggest load, and from me you shall have thorough and hearty cooperation. I will not let side issues draw me off from your main plans, in which I am to knock Joseph Johnston and to do as much damage to the resources of the enemy as possible." Cump's only concern was the subsistence of his army should it push deeply into enemy territory. "But that I must venture," he wrote. "Georgia has a million inhabitants. If they can live, we should not starve. If the enemy interrupt our communications, I will be absolved from all obligations to subsist on our own resources, and will feel perfectly justified in taking whatever and wherever we can find."

On May 4, 1864, the Army of the Potomac began its offensive, and the following day it struck Lee's army, fighting the two-day battle of the Wilderness. On May 5, Sherman's army marched out of its camps around Chattanooga, pointed for Atlanta. Gen. Joseph E. Johnston, with an army of some 62,000 men, stood opposed to Sherman's overwhelming force of 98,000 men. Sherman commanded three separate armies; The Army of the Tennessee, under General McPherson; the Army of the Cumberland, under General Thomas; and the Army of the Ohio, under Maj. Gen. John Schofield. Sherman would enjoy an almost three-to-two advantage over the enemy, and he would also have an advantage far more important. General Thomas's signal corps had broken the Confederate code back in Chattanooga, and Union signal men were able to read and translate Confederate messages as soon as they were sent. Thomas went so far as to have Confederate code books printed up for his signal corps officers. So, Sherman would commence his offensive with an advantage rarely seen in war. He would be privy to Joe Johnston's orders and would know the disposition, strength, and movements of the Confederate army as if they were being printed in his daily morning reports.

On May 7, Sherman made contact with Johnston's army north of Dalton, Georgia. Johnston had entrenched his army along the sides of a long, high mountain known as Rocky Face Ridge. The Confederate position was too formidable to risk a frontal assault, so Cump decided to demonstrate against the works while shifting a portion of his command around Johnston's left flank, in hopes of cutting the Confederate army off from its base in Atlanta. Elements of Sherman's army engaged the Confederates at Buzzard's Roost and Dug Gap, while General McPherson marched his Army of the Tennessee through Snake Springs Gap toward Resaca. McPherson reached the outskirts of the town on

May 9, only to find the enemy entrenched there. On May 10, Sherman determined to march the bulk of his army to join McPherson. Johnston, noting Cump's withdrawal from his front, retired south, toward Resaca, preparing once more to block Sherman's path toward Atlanta. This was the first in a series of maneuvers that was to define the Atlanta Campaign. Johnston, a master of defense, would take a strong position and invite Sherman to attack, in hopes of inflicting heavy casualties upon the Union army. Sherman, for his part, usually refused to oblige his adversary, and would maneuver around his flank, generally the Confederate left, attempting to interpose his army between Johnston and Atlanta. Johnston would interpret Cump's movements, appreciate the dangerous situation his army would be placed in if it were cut off from Atlanta, and would fall back to previously prepared defenses to repeat the scenario. What developed was a sort of military dance of maneuvering and counter-maneuvering across northwestern Georgia.

By May 13, Sherman and Johnston were facing one another, with their entire commands, at Resaca. The following day, Cump probed the Confederate defenses in a series of limited assaults, most of which were repulsed with high casualties. The probes were resumed on May 15, and Sherman assaulted with the corps of Generals Howard and Hooker. The Federal attack was thrown back by two Confederate divisions, with heavy losses, prompting Sherman to once more adopt a flanking movement around the Confederate left flank. The casualties sustained at Resaca were high, split pretty evenly between the opposing armies, with no real advantage gained by either side. Sherman attempted to envelop Johnston's position at Resaca, but the Confederate leader evacuated his army and marched it toward Atlanta, looking for a suitable place to make another stand.

Johnston retired toward Cassville. He noticed that the road to Cassville forked, with one fork going east, directly into the town. The other fork went south, to Kingston, before turning east to Cassville. Johnston correctly guessed that Sherman would be marching his columns over different roads in his approach, and felt there was an opportunity to defeat the Union army in detail while it was separated on its lines of march. But Sherman's troops did some hard marching and were able to rapidly concentrate to the north and west of Cassville before Johnston could spring his trap. Artillery was brought up, and the Southern

positions were heavily shelled. Johnston stated that Lt. Gens. John Bell
Hood and Leonidus Polk feared that Union artillery held a position to
enfilade their works, making them untenable. Johnston concluded that
he could not fight a major engagement when two of his three corps
commanders felt their lines could not be held. During the night of
May 19, Johnston abandoned his earthworks near Cassville and retired
further south.

Johnston fell back to Allatoona Pass, where he established a defensive line in the 1,000-foot mountains that dominated the area. Sherman had served in this region of Georgia 20 years before, as a young
lieutenant, and was well aware of the defensive possibilities the ridges
offered. Cump did not wish to sacrifice his army by throwing it in
hopeless charges against such a strong position, so he once more opted
to skirt around the Confederate left flank and make his way toward
Marietta. Johnston anticipated Sherman's move, and, on the night of
May 19, pulled his men out of their works and headed them once more
toward Atlanta. No major battles had been fought, but in the course of
two weeks, Sherman had maneuvered the Confederates out of several
formidable positions and compelled them to retreat ever closer to Atlanta. Indeed, Sherman had already covered half the distance between
Chattanooga and Atlanta.

Cump proposed to sever his link with the railroad and cross the
Etowah River. Orders were issued for 20 days' rations to be loaded on
wagons to provision the army until it could reach Marietta, where rail
service could be resumed. Upon crossing the river, Sherman's army
pointed in the direction of the little cross roads town of Dallas, Georgia.
Johnston once more anticipated Sherman's move and raced south to
block the Union forces. Cump had expected to find Dallas undefended,
but on the morning of May 25, he found the entire Army of Tennessee formed for battle behind freshly constructed earthworks, four miles
north of the town at New Hope Church. Gen. John Geary's division of
the Army of the Cumberland had been in advance when it made contact with the Confederates at 10:00 A.M. Geary's troops quickly routed
the Confederate skirmish line only to discover that John Bell Hood's
entire corps was in their front. To his dismay, Geary learned that his
lone division was now facing the entire Army of Tennessee. He immediately called off his attack and instructed his men to throw up log

breastworks. General Thomas had been riding with Geary and took control of the situation, sending a message back to hurry along General Howard's corps to the point of danger. Brig. Gen. Alphesus Williams's division was quick to respond, and his rapid arrival doubled the number of Union troops on the field. Thomas's position was still in grave danger, however, as his force was outnumbered by more than five-to-one. Williams command lost 800 men in 20 minutes of fighting, while Geary's command lost 500 men during the same time. Sherman had not yet grasped the seriousness of the situation and was perturbed by what he felt to be an unnecessary delay in his forward march. "I don't see what they are waiting for in front now," he snapped. "There haven't been twenty rebels there today." The unmistakable roar of musketry coming from that direction after Thomas's arrival alerted Cump to the reality that Johnston had stolen a march on him and was once more squarely positioned in his front.

By early afternoon, Hooker had joined Geary with his other two divisions. Hooker aligned his divisions for battle by placing them in column of brigades, meaning that the brigades of each division were stacked up one behind another. This formation provided maximum force for offensive punch, but it meant that each of the trailing brigades would be exposed to enemy fire without being able to respond from fear of hitting friendly troops in front of them. At 4:00 P.M., Hooker threw his divisions forward against a portion of the Confederate line held by Maj. Gen. Alexander P. Stewart's division, supported by three batteries of artillery. Hooker's force outnumbered Stewart's by more than three-to-one, but the Confederates were able to take advantage of the faulty alignment of the Union troops. More than 1,500 rounds of shell and canister were poured into the advancing Federals by the Southerners, each explosion creating huge gaps in the massed Union ranks. Hooker continued to press his attack for three hours, but the Union assault failed to gain the Rebel works. By 7:00 P.M., a heavy rain started to fall, and offensive operations were suspended. Hooker lost more than 1,600 troops in his abortive assaults, while the Confederates suffered less than half that number.

During the night of May 25 the remainder of Sherman's army arrived at New Hope Church and went into line opposite the Confederate's position. Cump reported that the "night was pitch-dark, it rained hard, and the convergence of our columns toward Dallas produced much confusion. I am sure similar confusion existed in the army opposed to us, for we were all mixed up. I slept on the ground, without cover, alongside of a log, got little sleep, resolved at daylight to renew the battle, and to make a lodgment on the Dallas Allatoona road if possible, but the morning revealed a strong line of entrenchments facing us, with a heavy force of infantry and guns." On May 28, McPherson's army was heavily assaulted while trying to shift to the right of Hooker. McPherson was able to repulse the attack, but was prevented from reaching his objective for three days. Sherman stated that "All this time a continual battle was in progress by strong skirmish-lines, taking advantage of every species of cover, and both parties fortifying each night by rifle-trenches, with head-logs, many of which grew to be as formidable as first-class works of defense."

On June 8, Sherman's army received reinforcements totaling 9,000 men, replacing his losses in the campaign, thus far, and meaning that his army still fielded the same number of men as it had upon leaving Chattanooga. The following day, the Federals found Johnston's army entrenched near Marietta, Georgia. Sherman probed the Confederate line and began shifting his army to flank the enemy. By June 18, Johnston was forced to withdraw his army to a new position to the west of Marietta, along a previously selected line at Kennesaw Mountain. The Western and Atlantic Railroad was the lifeline of the Confederate army, and from his position on Kennesaw Mountain Johnston could protect this vital link to Atlanta.

The Federal advance toward Atlanta had been rapid until it neared Marietta. Sherman's army had marched to a point only 22 miles from its objective, and it seemed as if nothing could stop it from pushing on to the gates of Atlanta. But the first two weeks of June witnessed almost constant rainfall that turned the roads into quagmires, making the deployment of troops almost an impossibility. It was also during this time that a reporter for the *New York Herald* discovered that the Union army was in possession of the Confederate code. The reporter submitted the story to his paper, and it was soon published. Confederate agents in New York promptly advised General Johnston that his code had been compromised, and it was accordingly changed. When Sherman learned what the reporter had done, he had the man arrested, and threatened to hang him as a spy. Sherman felt that he would have been within his rights to have executed the reporter, but his emotions eventually calmed, and in the end he decided to have the man banished to a quiet section of Ohio, never again to serve as a reporter with the army. For the remainder of the campaign, Sherman would be without the benefit of knowing the enemy's plans and dispositions.

Sherman was becoming frustrated with the delay at Kennesaw. He was eager to perform some great service that would justify the confidence Grant had shown in him by naming him to command in the West, and he viewed his campaign thus far to be less than expected. To be sure, Cump had maneuvered Johnston out of numerous strong positions and had forced him back to within 22 miles of Atlanta, but he had not succeeded in inflicting any serious damage on the Confederate army. He had not even fought any significant battles. The actions at Resaca, Dalton, and New Hope Church seemed little more than large skirmishes when compared with the battles of the Wilderness, Spotsylvania, and Cold Harbor that Grant had fought during the same period of time. Sherman even complained that the "whole attention of the country was fixed on the Army of the Potomac and that his army was completely forgotten." Irritated over the delay caused by the continual rains, as well as a lack of recognition for the achievements of his own army, Cump was moved to commit his one great blunder of the Atlanta Campaign. On June 25, he issued orders that a general assault be made upon the Confederate defenses on Kennesaw Mountain on June 27.

Kennesaw Mountain was actually two connected crests shaped like a foot. Big Kennesaw was 700-feet high, and resembled an ankle. Little Kennesaw was 100 to 150 feet lower than Big Kennesaw and was fashioned like a foot, extending 1,000 feet to the south, and ending in a series of small mounds. General Johnston's works lined the ridges of these two mountains, concealed by woods. The Confederate position was formidable, and Johnston felt that he could defend his lines against anything the Federals could throw at him. In fact, Johnston hoped Sherman would attack him at Kennesaw and batter his army against these strong defenses. Union reconnaissance of the works bore out Johnston's conviction, as no weak spot in the Southern lines could be found. It was eventually decided that the main Union attack would be made by the divisions of Maj. Gens. Jefferson C. Davis, John Newton,

David Stanley, and Absalom Baird. The choice was made not because any weakness had been found in the Confederate line, but because these four divisions happened to be the closest to the enemy.

At 8:00 A.M., on June 27, the divisions of Davis and Newton went forward, supported by Stanley and Baird, and preceded by a massive bombardment by over 200 pieces of Federal artillery. But the barrage had been ordered for only 15 minutes, and little real damage had been done to the Southern works. The Union infantry stepped out to cover the 600 yards to the enemy lines. They were greeted by a hail of musketry and artillery fire from the Confederates. Davis's and Newton's men went gallantly forward, despite the ever-increasing casualties, until they closed with the Confederates. In some places, Union forces actually breached the Southern lines, engaging in fierce hand-to-hand combat before being forced back. Once the attack had been repulsed, many Federal soldiers found themselves in a precarious position. Unable to advance or retreat, they were pinned down under the murderous fire of the enemy. General Thomas sent forward tools so that the trapped men might entrench themselves and gain some level of safety in their exposed positions, but the mere act of digging trenches caused the Union soldiers to become targets for the Confederate defenders. Cump wanted to renew the attack, but it was prevailed upon him that such a move would only result in needless losses. Sherman argued that "Our loss is small, compared to some of those (battle in the) East." General Thomas replied that "One or two more such assaults would use up this army." The level to which Sherman had come to view casualties was revealed in a letter written to Ellen a few days after the battle. "I begin to regard the death and mangling of a couple thousand men as a small affair, a kind of morning dash."

The assault had been a complete failure, resulting in a lopsided victory for the Confederates. Union losses were approximately 3,000, while Johnston's army had suffered only about one-third that number. Sherman was cured of his desire to make headlines, however, and never again would he consent to attack the Confederate army in prepared works. It is probable that this decision came not so much from a concern to avoid casualties as it did from a desire not to place himself in a position to lose another engagement. The day had not been a complete defeat for Sherman. In fact, on another part of the field events had

taken place that were to bode well for the Union. Gen. John Schofield
had been ordered to take his army to the right and exploit the Confederate left flank while the grand assault was being made on the Southern
lines. Schofield was successful in placing two brigades across Olley's
Creek, within five miles of the Chattahoochie River. Supported by
Maj. Gen. George Stoneman's cavalry, this meant that a sizable Union
force was now behind Johnston.

Cump determined to take full advantage of this success, and on
July 1 he ordered McPherson to move his army around the Confederate left, placing it in position alongside Schofield's. This movement
threatened to cut off Johnston's army from Atlanta, and the Confederate commander had no choice but to abandon his works and retire.
Sherman was sure that Johnston would retreat until he had crossed
the Chattahoochee River, using that natural barrier as his next defensive line. Cump was surprised when lead elements of his army ran
into Confederates four miles southeast of Marietta, at Smyrna, on
July 4. The Confederates were drawn up in line of battle, but Sherman
refused to oblige. The memory of Kennesaw Mountain was still too fresh
in his mind. Instead, he ordered Thomas to skirmish with the enemy
while McPherson and Schofield marched around the Confederate
left. The maneuver was successful, and Johnston once more was forced
to abandon his works and retire, this time to the west bank of the
Chattahoochee. Union forces pursued, and by sundown on July 5, John
Toomey, a soldier in the 27th Indiana, reported that they "were in sight
of Atlanta."

The position Johnston's army now occupied was described by Sherman as "one of the strongest pieces of field fortification I ever saw."
More than 1,000 slaves had been working for over two weeks to prepare it. The line was six miles long and one mile deep. Rifle pits were
supported by redoubts, 12-foot-thick forts made of logs and earth, with
artillery and heavy siege guns at intervals along the line. Sherman had
no intention of throwing his army against such a position and concluded to once again search for a way to maneuver the enemy out of his
works. Over the next few days, all of Sherman's commanders sent out
reconnaissance parties to search for a ford across the river. About eight
miles upriver from Johnston's position, a suitable ford was found at
Pace's Ferry by Gen. Thomas Wood, of the Army of the Cumberland.

General Thomas ordered pontoon bridges to be sent from Chattanooga, and by July 9 elements of Wood's division and Schofield's army were across the river and on the Atlanta side. When Johnston received word that he had been flanked, he prepared to cross the Chattahoochee and assume defensive positions closer to Atlanta. The Confederate commander expected to make his next stand at Peach Tree Creek. He secured seven heavy sea-coast artillery pieces, which had been added to the fortifications at this point. Johnston knew that Sherman must take Atlanta. There could be no more maneuvering once that city had been reached, and Johnston welcomed the prospect of finally getting to defend strongly prepared works against the frontal assaults of the Federal army.

The government in Richmond did not hold the same optimistic view as Johnston, however. Jefferson Davis had tracked the retiring of Johnston's army from Resaca with ever-increasing anxiety, and by the time the defenses at the Chattahoochee River had been evacuated, the Confederate president determined that the time for a change had come. Accordingly, he relieved Johnston of command on July 17, and replaced him with John Bell Hood, whose reputation as a hard-hitting commander had been earned while leading a division in Lee's Army of Northern Virginia.

Sherman was not familiar with Hood, and when he learned of the change in Confederate command he sought information about his new counterpart. General Schofield had attended West Point with Hood, and General Thomas had been his commander in the Second United States Cavalry before the war. These men provided Sherman with a profile of Hood that described the general as being "bold even to rashness and courageous in the extreme." Sherman was delighted with this intelligence. Hood would not be the sort of officer to wait to be attacked from behind prepared works, but would instead sally forth to become the attacker. If Sherman's assessment of the information was correct, a pitched battle would be imminent. In such a contest, the numerical superiority of the Federal army could be brought to bear for the first time since leaving Chattanooga.

Sherman did not have long to wait to find that his impressions of Hood were correct. On July 20, Hood attacked General Thomas's Army of the Cumberland while it was Crossing Peach Tree Creek. Five divisions of Confederate infantry were hurled at Thomas's men while they were astride the creek at approximately 4:00 P.M. The Federals were initially thrown back, and for a time it seemed as if they would be cut off from the rest of Sherman's army. But General Thomas responded quickly, assembling all available artillery in support of the sorely pressed infantry. The fury of the big guns, added to the musketry, proved sufficient to throw back the Southern assailants with heavy loss. While this fighting was taking place, Sherman was with McPherson and Schofield, in the vicinity of Decatur. Sherman intended to destroy the railroad from Decatur to Atlanta, and assumed that Hood would be compelled to come out of his defenses to protect his line of supplies. Sherman was so convinced that Hood would react as he planned that as Thomas's army was fighting for its life along the banks of Peach Tree Creek he sent orders that the Army of the Cumberland was to advance and capture the city, as there were "none of the enemy's troops between Peach Tree Creek and Atlanta." Sherman had been deceived. The only Confederate troops in front of McPherson and Schofield were a thin screen of cavalry belonging to Maj. Gen. Joseph Wheeler's command. Even after receiving reports from Thomas concerning the engagement at Peach Tree Creek, Sherman continued to delude himself as to the size of the enemy force in his front. "I have been with Howard and Schofield all of the day and one of my staff is just back from McPherson. All report the enemy in their front so strong that I was in hopes none was left for you." The reality was that Hood was throwing some 30,000 men against 20,000 Federals in Thomas's flank column. Cump had convinced himself that Hood's main force could not possibly be in front of Thomas, and even Thomas's reports of the extent of the engagement in his front could not change his mind-set. The Army of the Cumberland would have to fight it out alone against superior forces.

The Army of the Cumberland fought desperately against the repeated charges of the Confederates. By 6:00 P.M., Lt. Gen. William J. Hardee was forced to admit that the battle was stalemated. He ordered his reserve division, under the command of Maj. Gen. Patrick Cleburne, to join in the next attack, hoping to secure victory and destroy Thomas's army before darkness brought a close to the fighting. At this time Hardee received a message from Hood informing him that Schofield's force was within artillery range of Atlanta, and ordering

Hardee to send a division from his command to bolster the defenses of the city. Hardee responded by sending Cleburne's division, and though sporadic fighting continued along Peach Tree Creek until nightfall, the battle was ended. Hood had failed to achieve his objective of destroying Thomas's army while it was separated from the remainder of Sherman's force. The men of the Army of the Cumberland had inflicted 4,796 casualties on the enemy, while suffering only 1,710 of their own. This was Hood's best chance to drive the Federals back from the environs of Atlanta, but it ended in a crushing defeat for the Confederates because of the stand made by Thomas's army. Sherman would be the beneficiary of the Union victory and received credit for the accomplishment, but his actions on the field that day served as one of his worst performances during the entire war. He had become so convinced that Hood would react in the manner in which Sherman expected him to that he refused to admit that any other possibility existed. The Army of the Cumberland not only saved itself along the banks of Peach Tree Creek that day, but it also saved Sherman's reputation.

General Hood reorganized and refitted his army and prepared for another attempt to drive Sherman's army away from Atlanta. On July 22, just two days after the engagement at Peach Tree Creek, he assaulted General McPherson's Army of the Tennessee. Hood intended for General Cleburne's division to hold McPherson in place while Hardee's corps, supported by Wheeler's cavalry, marched around the left flank of the Federals to attack them in flank and rear. The assault was planned for the early morning of July 22, but Hood grossly underestimated the distance his troops would have to travel to get into position, and it was not until 1:00 P.M. until Hardee was in position to launch his attack. Hood's plan was to be further unraveled by the fact that Hardee was not on the Union flank, but was instead directly opposite Maj. Gen. Grenville Dodge's 16th Corps. The 16th Corps had been squeezed out of its line of march by the narrowness of the Atlanta approaches and had been forced to swing to the left of McPherson's main body. Hardee was unaware of this as he massed his troops for battle and still assumed that he had successfully flanked McPherson's forces. When he sent his regiments forward, it was straight into the waiting muzzles of Dodge's infantry. The engagement that would become known as the battle of Atlanta had begun.

Hardee's assault proved successful in the early going. The 16th Iowa Infantry was overpowered and forced to surrender. Maj. Gen. Giles Smith's division was driven from its fieldworks, and a number of Federal cannon were captured. General McPherson attempted to rally his men, but was killed. It looked as if Hardee might prevail, despite the fact he was attacking the Federals at a strong position and not on the flank. But Hardee was fighting alone. Cleburne was slow in getting his assault underway, and his division did not join in the attack until about 3:30 P.M. By that time, Hardee's troops were nearly spent. The battle continued until approximately 7:00 P.M., but each new Confederate thrust was thrown back in costly repulses. After six hours of fighting, Hardee called off the assault and withdrew his forces to Atlanta. The battle of Atlanta had proved to be another tragic loss for the Confederacy. Southern losses in the battle were 8,499, as opposed to Union casualties of 3,641. Hood had begun his offensive operations greatly outnumbered by Sherman's forces. After two bloody conflicts, he had only enlarged the disparity.

Sherman's actions during the battle of Atlanta showed the same alarming tendency that had come to the surface at Peach Tree Creek. At no time during the fighting did he order assistance to McPherson, leaving the Army of the Tennessee to fight it out alone against the Confederates. As Sherman himself put it, "if any assistance were rendered by either of the other armies the Army of the Tennessee would be jealous." The Army of the Tennessee had been his old command, and General McPherson was one of his favorite officers. He had ordered McPherson to move toward Decatur in the hope that Hood would attack him, and the honor of defeating the Confederate army would then belong to the Army of the Tennessee. This part of his strategy had all gone according to plan. But once the battle was joined, when its outcome was in serious doubt, to have allowed McPherson's army to wage the contest unsupported when Federal reinforcements were within striking distance seems a gross error in judgment that could have had tragic results for McPherson's army, and the Union forces as a whole. But the Army of the Tennessee held firm, just as the Army of the Cumberland had two days earlier, leaving Sherman to reap the accolades for a victory he played little part in.

On July 23, Sherman addressed the vacancy created in the command structure of the Army of the Tennessee by the death of General McPherson. Gen. Oliver O. Howard was assigned to the command of the army. Maj. Gen. Henry W. Slocum was then assigned to replace Hooker. As Sherman reorganized his army, he waited for Hood's next move. Cump knew that the fortifications around Atlanta were too strong to be carried by assault and hoped that cutting off the Confederate supply lines would compel Hood to either evacuate his lines or come out from behind his entrenchments to fight. Hood complied with Sherman's wishes on July 28 when he attacked Howard's army at Ezra Church with the corps of Gens. Stephen D. Lee and Alexander P. Stewart. The Confederate assaults were uncoordinated, with Lee assailing the Federals before Stewart's force was on the scene. Howard's troops threw up hastily fieldworks and fought a defensive battle against the Confederates. When Stewart reached the front, his numbers were added to the Southern attacks, but each was repulsed with bloody losses. By 5:00 P.M., the attack was called off and the Confederates retired toward Atlanta. This battle was the most lopsided defeat suffered by Hood's army, with the Confederates sustaining losses of 4,642 while inflicting only 700 casualties on the enemy. By assuming the role of the attacker, Hood had done in reverse what General Johnston had hoped to induce Sherman into undertaking. The Confederates had sustained some 18,000 casualties in making the three abortive assaults, and Hood's army no longer had sufficient numbers to meet Sherman in an open battle.

The disparity in manpower meant that all Hood could do was to crouch behind his works and hope that Sherman made a fatal mistake and attacked his strong defenses. Sherman had no such plan in mind, however. He would not subject his army to the losses required to take Atlanta's works by storm. Instead, he would lay siege to the city, and starve it into submission as he and Grant had done at Vicksburg. All of Hood's lines of supply would be cut, and there were no Confederate forces in the region to come to his aid. So far as Cump was concerned, it was only a matter of time before Atlanta was in Union hands. On August 28, the armies of Generals Thomas and Howard reached the Atlanta and West Point Railroad, 20 miles south of Atlanta, and began destroying Hood's last remaining line of supply. Hood realized what

Sherman was attempting and ordered the corps of Generals Hardee and Lee to attack the Federals around Jonesboro. On August 31, the last great act in the Atlanta Campaign was set in motion when Hardee's force attacked Howard. Howard's troops had seen the cloud of dust raised by Hardee's marching men when the Confederates were still some distance from Jonesboro and had quickly entrenched. When Hardee launched his attack, it was against a prepared position, and the result was a bloody repulse with 2,000 losses. Hardee had failed to drive the Federals away from the railroad and Hood was now out of options. To remain in Atlanta would mean sacrificing his army to no good advantage, so Hood decided to evacuate the city. On September 1, at 5:00 P.M., the Confederates marched out of the city, after destroying all of the military supplies that could not be taken with the army. On September 2, General Slocum's troops marched in to Atlanta to accept the surrender of the city from Mayor James M. Calhoun.

Sherman's four-month campaign was finally over. Atlanta was in Union hands. The loss of Atlanta also opened the heartland of the Confederacy to invasion by Sherman's army and opened the possibility that the Confederacy could be split again, as it had been when Vicksburg had fallen. The most important outcome of Sherman's capture of Atlanta was not of a military nature, however. War weariness had begun to grip the Northern citizenry in large measure during the summer of 1864. Grant's campaign in Virginia had witnessed tremendous battles, causing casualties never before seen in the war, but the Army of the Potomac seemed no closer to capturing Richmond than it had been when it stepped into the Wilderness in May. Sherman had been forcing the Confederate army in Georgia to give ground, but the prize of Atlanta had remained firmly in Confederate control. As the summer passed by, many in the North despaired of ever being able to defeat the Southern armies, and it looked increasingly as if the Democrats would win the presidential election to take place in the fall. The capture of Atlanta caused the Northern populace to instantly take heart, and to believe once more that the war could not only be won, but also that the end was in sight. By capturing Atlanta, Sherman had almost single-handedly ensured that Lincoln would be reelected in the November election and that the war would be fought through

Sherman at the works in front of Atlanta. The capture of this city boosted Northern morale to the extent that it all but ensured Lincoln's reelection as president. (Library of Congress)

to its final conclusion. For sheer importance, the capture of Atlanta was possibly the greatest service Sherman did for the Union during the entire war.

Sherman's objective at the beginning of the campaign was not only to seize Atlanta, but also to destroy the Confederate army defending that place. He had achieved the first of his objectives, but had not completed the second. To be sure, the Army of Tennessee had been whittled down in size to the point that it now numbered only about 40,000 men, slightly less than half the number of men in Sherman's army, but it was still in the field representing a threat to Sherman's forces. Hood had concentrated his army at Lovejoy's Station, approximately six miles south of Jonesboro. Sherman had no intention of pursuing the Confederates and bringing Hood's army to bay, however. Cump explained that "after due reflection, I resolved not to attempt at that time a further pursuit of Hood's army, but slowly and deliberately to move back, occupy Atlanta, enjoy a short period of rest, and to think well over the next step required in the progress of things."

Sherman allowed large numbers of furloughs to be granted to the men in his army following the capture of Atlanta, thus reducing the size of his army. Hood, on the other hand, was being reinforced in large measure. President Davis had ordered all Confederate troops along the Mississippi River to be transferred to Hood's command. Hood's numbers were also bolstered by the addition of numerous new recruits, and the return to the ranks of many veterans. Although Sherman still enjoyed a numerical advantage in manpower, it was no longer the two-to-one disparity that Hood had faced in front of Atlanta. The Gate City of the South had fallen to the Union, but the campaign was far from over. Sherman had to decide if the next phase would be the pursuit and destruction of Hood's army, or if another objective offered greater potential for bringing the war to a close. To this "next step required in the progress of things," he now devoted his full attention.

On September 9, Sherman wired Grant, asking permission to march his army east. Cump wished to drive his forces through the heart of Georgia, with the port city of Savannah being his final destination. He reasoned such a move would prove to the Southern citizenry that the Confederate government could no longer defend itself or protect them, and the resulting effect on Southern morale would have a great effect on bringing the war to a close. He proposed to destroy "roads, houses and people," and assured this commander, "I can make the march and make Georgia howl." Grant was hesitant to give permission for Sherman to proceed, but Cump quickly overcame his concerns and convinced him that he could successfully achieve the undertaking. The debate swirled for over a month, as the top command argued over the benefits and liabilities of a march to the sea, but in the end, Sherman prevailed when Grant acquired final approval for the move toward Savannah on October 11.

In the meantime, Sherman had been busy in Atlanta and northwestern Georgia. On September 11, he had agreed to a 10-day truce with General Hood for the purpose of removing all remaining civilians from Atlanta. Deciding that the city held no military significance for his army, Cump determined to waste no resources garrisoning the place. He also determined to make sure that Atlanta would be of no further benefit to the Confederates, so the city was to be destroyed. The remaining civilians were to be evacuated from the city before it was burned, and would be allowed to go north or south, depending upon their personal politics. Hood protested what he called Sherman's barbaric actions against noncombatants, but Cump refused to retract the order. "You might as well appeal against the thunder-storm as against these terrible hardships of war," he said in a response to Hood's pleas for leniency for the people of Atlanta. In the end, 446 families, all that remained of the more than 20,000 people who had once lived in Atlanta, were forced from their homes and became war refugees.

For his part, Hood was already putting in motion the strategy that he hoped would induce Sherman away from Atlanta and back into Tennessee. After receiving the refugees from Atlanta, the Confederate army marched southwest, around the flank of the Federals, before taking a course for the Tennessee River. Hood intended to operate against Sherman's line of supplies in Georgia, while the cavalry corps of Nathan Bedford Forrest did the same in Tennessee. Sherman responded by sending the Fourth Corps division of Maj. Gen. John Newton, along with the 14th Corps division of Brig. Gen. James D. Morgan, to

Sherman, as he appeared when preparing for his famous March to the Sea. (National Archives)

Tennessee to deal with Forrest. General Thomas, along with two corps, was dispatched to Chattanooga, to defend that place in the event that Hood tried to recapture the town. Thomas arrived on September 29, ahead of Hood, who was roughly retracing the route of operations the two armies had conducted in May and June. Shortly after arriving in Chattanooga, Hood cut Thomas's communications with Sherman, creating a period of uneasy watchfulness from the government in Washington.

Sherman pursued from Atlanta with five corps, but he did so at a leisurely pace that almost ensured he would not catch Hood. Cump seemed to be ignoring the Confederate army, and his attention was focused on Savannah, not northwestern Georgia or Tennessee. Thomas was to be left in charge of affairs in Tennessee, including the problem of dealing with Hood's army. Sherman would think no more about Hood, and was heard to say, "if he'll go the Ohio River, I'll give him rations." Once back in Atlanta, Sherman began to mold the army that would make the now famous March to the Sea. The 14th and 20th Corps from the Army of the Cumberland and the 15th and 17th Corps from the Army of the Tennessee, as well as John Schofield's Army of the Ohio were selected. This would give Sherman a fighting force of between 60,000 and 65,000 men. It also assured that he would have the cream of the crop from both armies under his command. When General Schofield showed no inclination to participate in the march, Sherman had the army redesignated as the 23rd Corps and assigned to Thomas.

The men who would be making this march were a mixture of veterans from the Eastern and Western Theaters of operations. The 11th and 12th Corps from the Army of the Potomac had been combined into the newly designated 20th Corps during the Atlanta Campaign, where it had fought as part of General Thomas's Army of the Cumberland. The 14th, 15th, and 17th Corps were all veterans of the Western Theater, having served from Mill Springs to Chickamauga. The two wings of the army would be commanded by Maj. Gens. Henry W. Slocum and Oliver O. Howard, and the 5,500 cavalry troopers that would accompany the army were under the command of Brig. Gen. Judson Kilpatrick. Slocum and Howard were both solid, dependable commanders, whose abilities to manage large bodies of troops on the battlefield had been

Sherman and his generals that would make the March to the Sea. Wing Commander Oliver O. Howard is standing on the far left of the photograph, to Sherman's right, while Sherman's other wing commander, Henry W. Slocum, is seated on Sherman's left. (National Archives)

tested on numerous fields of combat. Kilpatrick possessed a less favorable reputation and was a surprise choice for command of the cavalry. Graduated from West Point in the spring of 1861, Kilpatrick bore the distinction of being the first Union officer to be wounded in the war, when shot in the thigh at the battle of Big Bethel, in June of that year. By December 1862, he had risen to the rank of colonel in the cavalry and had begun the climb that would see him close his career in command of Sherman's cavalry. Highly ambitious and courageous to the point of being reckless, Kilpatrick had a tendency to order impressive but suicidal cavalry charges. Among his own men, he was nicknamed "Kill Cavalry" because of this penchant. In his mid-20s, he maintained his camps in a slovenly manner, and frequently availed himself of the many prostitutes he allowed to follow his command. In 1862, Kilpatrick was arrested and jailed on charges of corruption, for selling captured Confederate property for personal gain. He would be jailed a second time for a drunken spree in Washington, DC, and for accepting bribes from suppliers of horses to his command. He also had a reputation for cruelty to Southern civilians and was despised for his depredations committed against noncombatants. Cump was well aware of Kilpatrick's reputation. "I know that Kilpatrick is a hell of a damned fool," Sherman stated, "but I want just that sort of man to command my cavalry on this expedition." The March to the Sea was intended to further the individual ruin of the people of Georgia, and Sherman could think of no officer better qualified to visit destruction on the inhabitants of the state than Judson Kilpatrick.

Chapter 12

THE MARCH TO VICTORY

The end of October and the first two weeks of November were spent organizing and supplying the army to make its 300-mile march to Savannah. The Union force would consist of 60,000 infantry, 5,500 cavalry, and 60 pieces of artillery. Cump had ordered supply wagons "loaded with ammunition and supplies, approximating twenty days' bread, forty days' sugar and coffee, a double allowance of salt for forty days, and beef cattle equal to forty days' supplies." Sherman figured that this supply would get him deep into enemy territory, and he planned to forage for what his army needed from that point, "living chiefly if not solely upon the country, which I knew to abound in corn, sweet potatoes, and meats."

By November 15, all was in readiness. The army had been whittled down so that all of the troops that remained were in excellent fighting order. Indeed, Sherman's army was a picture of martial splendor. He had selected the finest units from the army that had made the campaign against Atlanta, and then had made sure that only the best among those units was finally accepted to make his march across Georgia. The campaign would take them through the heart of the Confederacy. They would be deep within enemy lines, cut off from any means of support from the Union, and completely on their own. It may have been appropriate that the march began with Sherman's army already somewhat cut off from the rest of the Union. Before leaving Atlanta, Sherman had taken steps to cut himself off from the rest of the North. He instructed his telegraphers to cut the lines leading into Chattanooga, in able to ensure that no eleventh-hour orders were received countermanding his intended march.

On the morning of November 15, Sherman's army marched out of what was left of Atlanta. The right wing, under the command of General Howard, moved southeast, toward Jonesboro. The left wing, under General Slocum, marched east, through Decatur and Stone Mountain, toward Madison. The objective of both wings was the state capital, at Milledgeville, but the divergent routes of the two wings had been selected to confuse the enemy. In this way, Sherman hoped to force the Confederates into splitting their force, instead of concentrating in front of his real objective. Cump remained in Atlanta on November 15, overseeing the final details of loading the wagons, as well as the final destruction of buildings in the city that could be used by the Confederate army. He would follow with the rearguard the next day.

At 7:00 A.M., on November 16, Sherman rode out of the city, "and reaching the hill, just outside of the old rebel works, we paused to look back upon the scenes of our past battles. We stood upon the very ground whereon was fought the bloody battle of July 22nd, and could see the copse of woods where McPherson fell. Behind us lay Atlanta, smoldering and in ruins, the black smoke rising high in the air, and hanging like a pall over the ruined city. Away off in the distance, on the McDonough road, was the rear of Howard's column, the gun-barrels glistening in the sun, the white-topped wagons stretching away to the south; and right before us the Fourteenth Corps, marching steadily and rapidly, with a cheery look and swinging pace, that made light of the thousand miles that lay between us and Richmond."

From the very first day, the march assumed the character that would define it to history. Sherman had ordered 15 miles per day the average distance covered by the marching columns, but reaching Savannah was not the only goal on Cump's agenda. The army had barely gotten outside of Atlanta before the real work of the campaign commenced. Bonfires could be seen all along the line of march, as eager soldiers set to the work of destroying anything that could be useful to the Confederate army. Of prime importance were the railroads, and these received the special attention of the troops. The men became quite adept at making what they called "Sherman's neckties" from the train rails. Wooden ties from the lines would be heaped in large piles and set ablaze. The metal rails would be placed on top of these bonfires until the center of the rails became red from the heat. Parties of men would then remove the rails, holding them by the ends, and bend them around telegraph poles, trees, or whatever else was at hand. This method of destruction ensured that the Confederates would not be able to employ rolling mills to straighten and reuse the rails. Sherman's troops became so skilled at this procedure that they could destroy a railroad while on the march, without failing to make their appointed distance of 15 miles per day.

The other signature feature of the March to the Sea that began as soon as the army cleared Atlanta was foraging. Sherman had left Atlanta with his wagons filled to the brim with supplies, and he intended to keep them overflowing with provisions. At daybreak, each brigade was authorized to send out a company of men, commanded by one or two officers, to scour the countryside on either flank of the marching column. Usually, these foraging details would range five miles or more from the main body, searching for plantations and farms. At each residence they came across, the work of collecting goods for the army would begin. Corn, forage, hams, and livestock of all varieties would then be confiscated, and wherever they were found, wagons and carriages would be taken to transport the seized property back to the army.

Slaves turned out in large numbers along Sherman's entire line of march. Viewing the Union troops to be their personal liberators, these slaves proved to be a ready source of intelligence and information for the army, and particularly for the foragers. They were quick to tell the soldiers where plantations and farms were located along the line of march and even informed the foragers where their masters had hidden goods in an effort to prevent their theft. Foragers delighted in this information, for it often led to the discovery of jewels, money, and other things of value that had been hidden or buried by their owners.

Sherman issued orders that the foragers confiscate only food and provisions necessary to sustain the army, and the theft of private property was forbidden. But neither Sherman, nor his officers, strictly enforced this order, and foragers regularly took anything that struck their fancy from terrified civilians unlucky enough to be within their range of operations. This range was indeed significant. Cump's army was marching along a line that was 60 miles long, and all Georgia residents living within that area were victims of Sherman's pledge to make Georgia howl.

The Confederate military had precious few resources with which to oppose Sherman's horde of Union invaders. Lt. Gen. William J. Hardee, in command of the Department of South Carolina, Georgia, and Florida, was faced with an overwhelming task. Hardee was woefully undermanned to protect a department that encompassed three states. In Georgia, he had the 10,000 man garrison force that occupied Savannah. These troops had been protecting the port city for the duration of the war, however, and had yet to see combat. There was also the 10,000 man cavalry division of Maj. Gen. Joseph Wheeler. The only other force available to Hardee was Maj. Gen. Gustavus W. Smith's Georgia Militia, numbering some 3,000 men. With a total force of just over one-third the number of men in Sherman's army, and with only a fraction of those being combat veterans, Hardee was almost powerless to prevent Sherman's army from marching wherever it pleased. The best he could hope to do was harass and impede the enemy and continue to press Richmond for reinforcements it did not have.

On November 22, the first real fighting of the campaign took place at Griswoldville, Georgia, outside of Milledgeville, when Judson Kilpatrick's cavalry, riding in advance of the infantry, made contact with Wheeler's troopers. Kilpatrick and Wheeler were both supported by infantry, and in the end, the Confederates were compelled to retire from the field with heavy losses. Union casualties in the day's fighting amounted to only 94, while the Confederates had suffered a total of 1,123 losses. The following day, on November 23, Sherman's forces marched into Milledgeville, capturing the state capital. Sherman and his officers held a mock session of the Georgia Legislature in the state capitol, jokingly voting Georgia back into the Union.

Over the next several days, Wheeler's cavalry clashed with Kilpatrick in a series of rearguard actions. Skirmishes took place at Ball's Ferry on November 24–25 and at Sandersville on November 25–26.

Kilpatrick had been ordered to attempt the liberation of Union prisoners being held at Camp Lawton, in Millen, but this was abandoned when information was received that the prisoners had been moved to another location. On November 28, Kilpatrick was surprised and nearly captured when Wheeler's troopers attacked the Union force at Buck Head Creek. The Confederates forced Kilpatrick to give ground, but were severely punished by the rearguard action of the Fifth Ohio Cavalry. Union losses in the engagement were only 46, while the Confederates suffered approximately 600 casualties. Kilpatrick had been compelled to withdraw, but Wheeler had once more suffered a disparity in losses he could ill afford.

President Lincoln kept a daily vigil for news of the army, fearing that it may be swallowed up in the Georgia interior. Lincoln had no intelligence concerning the limited forces available to General Hardee, and imagined that the Confederacy still had sufficient resources to concentrate against Sherman that could cut his army off and force it to surrender. With no positive news to allay his anxiety, Lincoln could only watch and wait. If the president could have seen Cump's veterans feasting on cured hams, fresh chickens, and every delicacy afforded by the region, if he could have heard the laughter and boasts coming from every Union camp, he would have realized how unfounded was his apprehension over the safety of "Uncle Billy's Boys."

By December 10, Sherman's army had reached the outskirts of Savannah. In little more than three weeks he had marched through 300 miles of Georgia, leaving a path of destruction 60 miles wide. 18,000 square miles of Georgia's heartland had been laid ruin, as Cump fulfilled his promise to Grant and Lincoln to make the citizens of the South feel the war in all its horrors and depredations. Just before reaching the city, however, one of the most heartrending events of the campaign was played out. Sherman's march had, by its mere nature, liberated thousands of slaves from bondage. Many of these ex-slaves felt that their only chance to stay free was by keeping in close proximity to the Federal army. Once the Yankees had marched on, it was feared that they would be taken into custody and once more commuted to slavery. Sherman had pleaded with the blacks not to encumber his army with thousands of refugees that would slow down the pace of his march and siphon away food needed by his troops. Many of the recently freed slaves heeded his advice, but many could not be convinced to abandon their liberators. Thousands followed in the wake of the army. Some of the men were employed as teamsters, or to do manual labor, but the women, children, and elderly were forced to beg the soldiers for food. As the army neared Savannah, the plantations and farms that had served to supply Sherman's needs became scarce, and foraging details were returning to camp with ever decreasing amounts of provisions. Maj. Gen. Jefferson C. Davis was becoming irritated by the throng of refugees trailing in the rear of his column, and he determined to do something about it. When Davis's corps approached the Ebenezer Creek, orders were issued for the engineers to use pontoons to bridge the 165-foot span. Once the bridge was completed, Davis crossed his troops. The ex-slaves that were following were told that they must not cross the span as a fight with the enemy was expected on the opposite shore, and a guard was placed to make sure they complied. Once the last of Davis's soldiers was across, the guard was ordered to take up the bridge as they moved to the opposite shore, thus trapping the refugees at the water's edge. Joe Wheeler's cavalry had been nipping at the heels of Davis's command throughout the day, and it was well known that Confederate horsemen were in the general vicinity. When the blacks realized what was taking place, they were seized with terror. Many jumped into the creek in an attempt to flee capture or death at the hands of the Confederates, but drowned because they didn't know how to swim.

Sherman found his approach to Savannah blocked by acres of flooded rice fields. General Hardee ordered the fields to be flooded to provide a natural barrier for the city. His 10,000 troops were placed behind strong earthworks, making it a formidable task for Sherman to pry them out. Because of the flooding, Sherman's troops would have to attack the city over narrow causeways that could be easily defended by the outnumbered Confederates. Unwilling to risk the losses that would accompany such an attack, Cump cast about to find if there was a way to maneuver Hardee out of his entrenchments. Most importantly, he needed to make contact with the Union fleet under the command of Rear Admiral John A. Dahlgren. Dahlgren's fleet carried food and supplies that were now sorely needed by Sherman's men. Several days ago, a few volunteers slipped by the Confederates in a canoe to make contact with Dahlgren and inform him that Sherman's army had reached Savannah. Now, the only question was how to deal with Hardee's command so as to open a ready line of communication with the fleet.

Cump determined to make Fort McAllister, just south of Savannah, his primary objective. The fort was situated along the banks of the Ogeeshee River and would provide easy access to the ocean and Dahlgren's ships. The large guns of the fort all pointed out to sea, to defend against a naval attack, and Sherman was sure that the works were susceptible to an infantry assault by land. Accordingly, he ordered General Howard to detach a division from his command to storm the fortifications. Brig. Gen. William B. Hazen's division was selected. On December 13, General Hazen got his division in position to make the attack shortly before nightfall. The fort was defended by Maj. George Anderson and a garrison of only 230 men. Hazen's men charged across open ground lined with abatis and mined with torpedoes. The defenders did their best to contest Hazen's advance, but within 15 minutes the fighting was over and the fort was in Union hands. Communications with the fleet were established and Sherman could now prepare for the siege and capture of Savannah. According to Lincoln, Sherman's army had gone into a hole at Atlanta. It had now emerged from that hole, on the Atlantic Coast.

With the capture of Fort McAllister Sherman could now turn his full attention to the investment of Savannah. He sent a request for surrender to General Hardee, which was adamantly declined. Although Cump's army was far superior to Hardee's, the thought of flinging it against the prepared Confederate works did not sit well with Sherman. Instead, the city was to be taken by siege, as had been done at Vicksburg. The Federal army already walled off the city from three sides, and the only route still open to Hardee's command lay to the east. Sherman took steps to close off this avenue of escape by enlisting the assistance of General Foster's forces at Hilton Head. Cump desired to have the division of Brig. Gen. John P. Hatch ferried down to Savannah, where it would close off the Old Dike Road, leading into South Carolina. Cump went to Hilton Head to personally confer with General Foster and received his hearty support for the plan. On the night of December 20, Cump was on his way back to Savannah when the ship he was traveling on went aground. The operation to close off the Old

Dike Road was too late. Hardee had escaped into South Carolina during the early morning hours of December 21, leaving Savannah in Union hands. The Confederates had escaped with all their troops and light artillery, but all of the heavy ordnance, along with great quantities of public and private goods were left behind. Cump reported the event in a telegraph to Washington: "To His Excellency, President Lincoln; I beg to present you as a Christmas gift, the city of Savannah, with one hundred and fifty heavy guns and plenty of ammunition, and also about twenty-five thousand bales of cotton."

Lincoln responded on December 26, "My Dear General Sherman, many, many thanks for your Christmas gift—the capture of Savannah."

The wanton destruction that had characterized the March to the Sea was abandoned once the army occupied Savannah. The city was to be spared the devastation that had marked Sherman's 60-mile-wide march through the state, as the victors seemed in a magnanimous mood. Work was begun to clear the harbor of mines and obstructions that kept the Union blockading fleet outside its entrance, and captured Confederate stores were collected for disbursement or shipment north. Private property was held strictly off limits to the troops, and with a fleet of ships, filled with supplies, anchored off shore, the practice of foraging was suspended.

Sherman now turned his attention to President Lincoln's question of "what next?" Grant was with the Army of the Potomac, locked in daily combat with Lee's Army of Northern Virginia at Richmond and Petersburg. Lee's army, at this time, was the only military organization of any significant size available to the Confederacy. All were certain that if Lee's army was to be destroyed, the end of the Confederacy would follow shortly. Initially, Grant had planned for Sherman to embark his army on ships and sail to Virginia, where it could assist the Army of the Potomac in subduing Lee's forces. Sherman had proposed that his army take an overland route, north through South Carolina and North Carolina, eventually placing him in the rear of Lee's forces. Along the way, he could visit the same sort of destruction and devastation upon the Confederate citizenry as had been shown to the people of Georgia, further weakening the Southern resolve. Grant approved of Cump's plan, stating that his march through the Carolinas would also serve to prevent the Confederates from collecting a force together that could oppose him. On January 2, 1865, Sherman received orders from Grant authorizing him to conduct an overland campaign as soon as he accumulated sufficient supplies to do so. January 15 was the date selected to begin the march.

Heavy winter rains caused extensive flooding in the Savannah area, and turned the roads into rivers of mud, forcing Sherman to delay the start of the campaign by two weeks. On February 1, the campaign to march through the Carolinas and the war began. Cump's army would march in two wings, commanded by Generals Slocum and Howard, just as it had across Georgia. Slocum's wing took the interior path, to the left, while Howard's wing occupied the right. Slocum's wing threatened Augusta, while Howard's wing threatened Charleston. Columbia, the capital of South Carolina, was Sherman's real target, but his lines of march confused the Confederates and kept them from massing at his true objective.

Only minor delaying actions took place in the march through South Carolina. Sherman's troops took possession of Columbia on February 17. Most of the city was in smoldering ruins, having burned to the ground in a great fire that is still the object of controversy and discussion. Southern allegations charge that drunken Union soldiers were responsible for torching the city, but the most probable explanation is that the flames from the cotton bales were responsible for the conflagration. Sherman stated that he never gave an order to have Columbia burned, but he was not sorry it happened. It is easy to understand why Southerners would affix blame for the destruction on the Union army. Sherman's troops took special vengeance on the people of South Carolina ever since they had crossed into the state from Savannah. To most Northerners, South Carolina had played a leading role in bringing about the war. The state had been the first to secede from the Union, blazing a path for the rest of the states of the deep South. The first hostile action to take place had also been when Confederate forces fired on the defenders of Fort Sumter in Charleston Harbor. Rightly or wrongly, most of Sherman's troops blamed South Carolina for the years of warfare that had followed Fort Sumter, and now they were intent on making the state pay. Foraging parties were once more sent out into the countryside, and the resultant theft and wanton destruction done against Confederate civilians surpassed that which had taken place in Georgia.

As demoralizing as Sherman's policy of destruction to South Carolina was to Confederate leaders, the pace of his march proved to be even more upsetting. Southerners were sure that the winter rains would greatly hamper the Federal's march, and that numerous streams and rivers that bisected the region would prove to be natural obstacles to his advance. But Sherman's troops covered an average of 10 miles per day, regardless of conditions or natural barriers. Muddy roads were corduroyed with logs almost as fast as the army could march, and streams and rivers were spanned with pontoon bridges with amazing speed. The ease with which the Federals traversed the Carolina countryside did as much to deflate Confederate morale as any action of Sherman's army. To most, it seemed as if the Federal army was truly a resistless tide that could not be stopped. Confederate Gen. Joseph E. Johnston offered the greatest compliment to his old adversary when he stated, "There had been no such army since the days of Julius Caesar."

Johnston's evaluation of Sherman's army held personal as well as professional meaning. Johnston had been restored to field command on January 25, at the urging of Robert E. Lee, the newly appointed general-in-chief of the Confederate army. His new command encompassed the departments of Florida, Georgia, South Carolina, North Carolina, and Southern Virginia. From the widely dispersed remnants of Confederate forces within his department, it was hoped that Johnston could gather together an army capable of stopping Sherman's advance. The mission was daunting, and the limited resources available to Johnston made it look all but impossible, especially since he would have to contend with an enemy army that he himself rated as being one of the finest ever assembled. By the time Johnston collected together his forces, he would have approximately 20,000 troops under his command. The majority of these were the garrison troops from Savannah and Charleston, led by General Hardee. The garrison force from Wilmington, North Carolina, made up mainly of Maj. Gen. Robert F. Hoke's division from the Army of Northern Virginia would be added to Hardee's troops, as would the remnants of the Army of Tennessee, numbering only 4,000 to 5,000 men, now under the command of Lt. Gen. Alexander P. Stewart. Johnston would call his new command the Army of the South, and what it lacked in manpower if fully made up for in leadership. Three of the full generals of the Confederate army would be serving with the

Army of the South. In addition to Johnston, would be Braxton Bragg
and P.G.T. Beauregard.

Johnston's forces were still widely separated when Sherman's army
crossed into North Carolina on March 9, 1865. General Hardee, along
with Hampton's and Wheeler's cavalry, was fighting a delaying action against the Federal army. Braxton Bragg was 150 miles away, near
Goldsboro, North Carolina. Gen. John Schofield was in Wilmington,
with 20,000 troops, poised to support Sherman as he moved northward
through the state. His first objective would be Goldsboro. Johnston
found himself in the unenviable position of having Grant's Army of
the Potomac to his rear, Schofield's army on his flank, and Sherman's
army in his front. Once his forces were concentrated, Johnston could
do little against the overwhelming numbers arrayed against him. The
most he could hope for was to defeat a portion of the Union forces if he
could find them isolated from support.

One of Johnston's first objectives was to prevent Schofield and Sherman from joining forces. When Bragg reported a Union force moving
inland from New Bern toward Goldsboro and requested reinforcements, Johnston felt that an opportunity to achieve this objective was
at hand. The Union troops, some 12,000 strong, were commanded by
Maj. Gen. Jacob D. Cox. Bragg had only about 8,500 troops in his
command, but he attacked Cox near Kinston on March 7. Initially,
the battle went well for the Confederates, and an entire regiment from
Maj. Gen. Samuel P. Carter's division was captured. Southern victory
was at hand when Bragg detached a portion of his attack force to meet
a Federal threat that proved to be fictitious. General Cox used this time
to bring up his reserve division and turned the tide of the battle. Union
losses at Kinston were 1,101, while Confederate casualties amounted to
1,500 troops sorely needed by Johnston.

Meanwhile, troopers under the command of Wade Hampton and
Joe Wheeler attacked Kilpatrick's command on March 10 at Monroe's
Crossroads, south of Fayetteville, in what was to be the last all-cavalry
battle of the war. The Confederates attacked at dawn, catching many
of the Union troopers sleeping. General Kilpatrick was in a nearby
log cabin with a mistress when the Southern troopers assaulted and
fled the scene in his nightshirt to hide in a swamp. After regaining his
composure, he returned to reorganize his routed troopers. The Federal

counterattack eventually drove Hampton and Wheeler from the field. The Confederates had inflicted 183 casualties on Kilpatrick's command while only suffering 86 themselves. More importantly, the action at Monroe's Crossroads delayed the Federal army sufficiently to allow Confederate infantry at Fayetteville to conduct an organized crossing of the Cape Fear. On March 11, Sherman's forces marched into Fayetteville and took possession of the city.

Cump allowed his troops to rest for a few days in Fayetteville. The rain that had been a constant throughout the campaign continued as the Federal army stepped out for what was hoped to be the final leg of the journey to Virginia. General Hardee, at Averasboro, found himself in a dilemma because of this advance. The rains had caused the Black River to become swollen to the point that his wagon train could not cross. Hardee was faced with abandoning his train or turning about to face Sherman's troops, hoping to hold them off long enough for his wagons to cross the raging torrent. Hardee chose the latter. Deploying his troops into a defensive position containing four lines, he duplicated the battle plan Gen. Daniel Morgan had employed at the battle of Cowpens in the Revolutionary War. General Kilpatrick's cavalry ran into Hardee's position on the afternoon of March 15, but withdrew after feeling out his defenses. At dawn on March 16, Hardee launched an attack on Alpheus Williams' XX Corps of Slocum's left wing, even though Hardee's command numbered less than 6,000, as opposed to the almost 26,000 in Slocum's wing. The Confederates enjoyed initial success, driving back the Federals until Williams moved up reinforcements and counterattacked. The Federals pushed forward, capturing two of Hardee's defensive lines before being stopped cold at the third. The fighting lasted several hours by the time Jefferson Davis's XIV Corps arrived on the field, but swampy fields prevented Davis from deploying his corps for combat before darkness brought an end to the fighting. Fearing being flanked by Davis's forces, and already having bought enough time for his wagons to cross the Black River, Hardee retreated that night toward Smithfield, where General Johnston was concentrating his army. Casualties at Averasboro totaled approximately 1,500 for both sides, but Hardee had been able to delay the advance of Slocum's left wing for almost two full days, causing it to become separated from Howard's wing.

This separation created just the sort of opportunity Johnston had been hoping for. It might be possible for the Army of the South to fight a portion of Sherman's army in detail before reinforcements could arrive from the other wing. Intelligence from Wade Hampton stated that the head of Slocum's wing would be a full day's march from the head of Howard's wing by the time Slocum reached the hamlet of Bentonville, 16 miles south of Smithfield. Hampton also informed Johnston that the ground around Bentonville offered an excellent position for his army to fight a battle against Slocum's wing. Accordingly, Johnston ordered all of his troops to concentrate at Bentonville for the decisive battle of the campaign.

But Hampton's intelligence was faulty. Maps used by both sides were antiquated and did not show roads built in the previous decade. They were also inaccurate concerning proper distances between points. Sherman's wings were not separated by a full day's march. In reality, the gap between the two wings was only half that much, and Howard's wing would be within easy supporting range of Slocum. In addition, Slocum's troops were actually closer to Bentonville than the various elements of Johnston's army. If Johnston was to defeat Slocum's wing, he would have to do so in one grand rush. Any prolonged fighting would give Howard's men ample time to march to Slocum's support. He would also have to beat Slocum to Bentonville. Had Johnston been aware of the true state of affairs, it is doubtful if he would have consented to make a stand there.

For his part, Sherman was aiding Johnston in springing a trap on Slocum's wing. Cump had become blinded by the success he had already achieved in the campaign and refused to believe that the Confederates were capable of mounting any resistance to his march. In his memoirs, he would write, "All signs induced me to believe that the enemy would make no farther opposition to our progress, and would not attempt to strike us in the flank while in motion." Rumors of a Confederate concentration were discounted, and when Brig. Gen. William Carlin reported to his corps commander, Jefferson Davis, that a local farmer along his line of march reported an enemy buildup and feared that a battle might be fought on his land, Davis passed along the information to Sherman. Cump discounted the intelligence, telling Davis, "No, Jeff, there is nothing there but . . . cavalry," and ordering him to "Brush them out of the way in the morning."

Slocum's troops reached Bentonville before Johnston could con-centrate his army on the field. Wade Hampton's cavalry was on the ground, and as soon as he received confirmation from Johnston that the rest of the army was on its way, Hampton determined to hold his position. On the morning of March 18, Hampton engaged the Federal advance in brisk skirmishing, lasting throughout the afternoon. His troopers slowly gave ground until they reached a farm owned by the Cole family. Here, Hampton dismounted his troopers, placing them in line along the edge of a grove of woods, and brought up his artillery. Hampton knew that if Slocum ordered a general assault against his position, he would be swept away by the force of superior numbers, but he gambled that the game of bluff he was playing would buy sufficient time for Johnston to arrive.

The ruse was successful. By the time the Federals got into position to attack Hampton's works it was almost sunset. Hampton had used the time the Federals took in preparing for an assault to materially strengthen his works, and in the twilight they seemed quite formidable to the attackers. Not knowing the strength of the defenders, it was de-cided to postpone the attack until the following morning, when there would be more daylight for the operation. By the next morning, John-ston would have a line of infantry solidly emplaced in the defenses, and Slocum's wing would be facing the Army of the South.

Sunday, March 19, dawned bright and sunny, as the rains gave way to a beautiful early spring day. Union and Confederate cavalry resumed their skirmishing at first light, while Sherman's infantry listened to the sounds of band music and prepared their breakfast. Cump had been riding with the left wing for the past several days, and following an early breakfast he prepared to depart for Howard's wing. Before leaving, Sherman met with Generals Slocum and Davis at a crossroads near the Union biv-ouac. All three officers were mounted, and the topic of discussion was the route of march toward Goldsboro. General Davis expressed concern over the volume of skirmishing at the front, stating that he felt some-thing was amiss. Sherman was convinced that the Confederates were whipped and would not fight. Insisting that there was nothing in the path of Slocum's wing but dismounted cavalry, he advised Davis to brush them out of the way and continue his march. With that, Cump and his staff bid farewell to Slocum and Davis and started off for Howard.

General Davis sent forward the division of Brig. Gen. William P. Carlin to drive the supposed Confederate cavalry off. Carlin was supported by Brig. Gen. Absalom Baird's division. When Carlin struck the Southern line it was soon evident that it was being held by more than dismounted cavalry. The Confederates were there in force, and the fieldworks were held by infantry. Carlin formed his battle line and attempted to brush the defenders out of the way, as Cump had instructed, but soon discovered that the job was too much. The Union attacks were repulsed, with heavy losses, throughout the morning. As the Union units fell back from their abortive assaults, they began to throw up hasty fieldworks, in defense against a counterattack, while Slocum moved up the division of Brig. Gen. James D. Morgan and placed it on the right of his line. Morgan's men began at once to prepare strong fortifications, digging trenches, topped with head logs. Morgan's preparation would prove to save the Union army from a humiliating defeat later in the day. Slocum sent word back to the XX Corps to make its way to the battlefield with all possible haste.

General Howard heard the sounds of the battle as his wing marched toward the Neuse River. Fearing that Slocum had encountered serious difficulty, he sent a messenger to inform Slocum he could feel free to call upon the XV Corps for reinforcement. Receiving no response to this message, he dispatched his chief of artillery to personally convey his offer of support. This officer ran into Sherman along the road, after traveling only a few miles from Howard's camp. Sherman informed him that he had just come from Slocum's position and that there was nothing there but a division of Confederate cavalry. The messenger, thus informed, returned to the right wing without delivering the message. More importantly, the XV Corps continued to march forward, increasing the distance between itself and Slocum.

With two Union divisions already repulsed, and a third on the field, General Johnston planned to administer a knockout punch designed to eliminate Davis's XIV Corps and cripple Slocum's left wing. General Hardee arrived on the field with his forces following the morning fight, and Johnston army was now fully concentrated. The Confederate commander ordered a full-scale attack against Davis's corps, hoping to sweep his three divisions from the field, and throw them back upon the divisions of Williams' XX Corps, still en route to Bentonville. In the resulting confusion, Johnston was sure that he would be able to route both corps and inflict enough casualties that Slocum's wing would be crippled and unable to offer significant assistance when he then turned to face Howard's wing.

At 3:00 P.M., Johnston ordered his battle lines forward, in what was to be the last great Confederate infantry charge of the Civil War. The Confederates crushed the Union left flank and nearly captured General Carlin. The Union center was pushed back, and it seemed for a while as if Johnston's plan was going to work. But Morgan's division on the Union right was holding firm. This division stood between General Johnston and the completion of his plan should have been overwhelmed by superior Confederate forces. But Johnston was having trouble coordinating his attacks. His commanders were sending in their units piecemeal, instead of massing for a grand charge, and Morgan's men were able to beat off each of the fragmented attacks. By the time the Confederate commanders took control of the situation and prepared a concentrated assault, elements of the XX Corps had arrived on the field and taken up positions to support Morgan. Although fighting into the night, Johnston's opportunity had passed. In the morning, Slocum's entire wing would be on the field. Howard's wing would also arrive at Bentonville on March 20, presenting Johnston with a disparity in numbers of more than three to one.

March 20 dawned to find Johnston's army and Slocum's wing each behind field works, facing one another across a no man's land. Although there were no large-scale attacks initiated by either side, the day witnessed frequent bouts of skirmishing and almost continual sniping. Howard's wing began reaching the field afternoon, meaning that Johnston was hopelessly outmatched. Sherman was now on the field in person. The opportunity to destroy a portion of Sherman's army had passed. Johnston could not hope to assume the role of the aggressor against Cump's combined forces and risked the possibility of being cut off from his line of retreat and losing his entire army by remaining at Bentonville. But Johnston remained. Officially, he stated that he had held his line on March 20 in order to gather all his wounded from the field. It is probable that he also stayed because he hoped that Sherman would take the offensive to launch a general attack, giving him the opportunity to administer a repulse to the Union army as he had done at

Kennesaw Mountain. But Cump would not be goaded into making such a frontal attack. In fact, Sherman seemed hesitant to fight at all at Bentonville. He had the last major Confederate army of any significance in the West trapped, and with his superiority in numbers should have been able to overpower and eliminate Johnston's army once and for all. Instead of planning for a decisive fight, however, Cump's thoughts were of resuming his march for Goldsboro.

March 21 found the two armies still facing one another. Heavy skirmishing and artillery duels marked the day, but no general assault was planned by either side. Maj. Gen. Joseph A. Mower requested permission to make a reconnaissance of his front, and General Blair granted his request, not knowing that Mower planned to accomplish more than merely scouting the Confederate position. Mower intended to mount an attack against the left flank of Johnston's line. Mill Creek ran to the rear of the Confederate position and had become swollen by the recent rains. Johnston's only avenue of escape was the Mill Creek Bridge, and Mower sought to cut the Confederates off from the bridge so that the entire army could be destroyed or captured. On the afternoon of March 21, Mower moved forward on a two brigade front. Johnston's left was thinly held by Joe Wheeler's dismounted cavalry, which was easily driven back by Mower's infantry. The attack surged forward, capturing Johnston's headquarters, and nearly capturing the general himself. The Union troops advanced to within 50 yards of Mill Creek Bridge, when they were counterattacked by a hastily gathered reserve, under the command of General Hardee. Mower's men fell back, but reorganized to make another attempt against the bridge. This attempt was called off by Sherman. Mower had come closer than Cump ever imagined to trapping the entire Confederate army.

On the night of March 21, General Johnston evacuated his position and made good his escape across Mill Creek Bridge. The three days of fighting at Bentonville had resulted in more than 4,000 casualties to both sides, with the Confederates suffering over 2,500 of that total. Already severely outnumbered, and with his ranks now thinned by the losses at Bentonville, Johnston withdrew to Smithfield to reorganize and lick his wounds. Sherman mounted no pursuit of the enemy. After scouting Johnston's army to determine its location, the Federal army made plans to resume its march for Goldsboro, where General

Schofield with 20,000 reinforcements and much needed supplies awaited. No one on either side could have known it, but the last battle of the campaign had been fought at Bentonville.

Upon reaching Goldsboro, Sherman allowed his men a well-deserved period of rest. Cump received the congratulations of General Grant and was instructed to come to Grant's headquarters, at City Point, for a personal meeting to discuss the final operations of the war. Cump arrived on March 27 for a two-day meeting between himself, Grant, and President Lincoln. Sherman proposed to march his army north to join with Grant against Lee's Army of Northern Virginia. Grant declined this proposal, fearing that the approach of Sherman's army would cause Lee to evacuate his defenses and flee. Above all, Grant wished to prevent Lee and Johnston from joining forces, and felt that circumstance might be realized should Sherman march toward Virginia. Grant wanted Sherman to make Johnston's army his primary objective. He was to march directly for Johnston, at Smithfield, to engage and hopefully destroy the enemy. April 10 was set for the date the campaign was to begin.

Sherman's army, now more than 100,000 strong, stepped out on the morning of April 10 for what most felt would be the final campaign of the war. Johnston, at Smithfield, had received prior warning of Sherman's movements and evacuated his army toward Raleigh before the Federals arrived. The Army of the South had also increased in numbers since the battle of Bentonville, but the 35,000 men Johnston had under his command were still no threat to the massive Union army confronting them. Neither commander knew that Robert E. Lee had surrendered at Appomattox Courthouse the previous day, and that Johnston's army was the last significant military force remaining in the Confederacy. Johnston withdrew toward Raleigh, and skirmishing took place at the town between his rearguard and Sherman's advance. By April 12, both commanders had received intelligence about the surrender of Lee's army. General Johnston weighed his options. He could march his army south, back into Georgia, where the war could be prolonged by weeks or even months. He could disband his army and continue the war guerrilla style, but that would bring further misery and destruction to the South. Feeling that the Confederacy was defeated and that further resistance would result in useless bloodshed, Johnston sent a message to Sherman asking for a meeting to discuss terms of surrender for his army.

On April 17, Sherman and Johnston met at the home of James Bennett, near Durham Station, to discuss the capitulation of Johnston's army. Cump received notification of the assassination of President Lincoln just before he left for the meeting. Fearing the effect the news might have upon the peace initiative, Cump ordered that the news not be given to the troops until his return. When Sherman met with Johnston, he advised him of Lincoln's death. None of the Confederates had known of Lincoln's assassination, and the news was greeted with profound professions of regret. Johnston and his staff voiced the opinion that Lincoln's death was as much a tragedy for the people of the South as it was for the Northern populace because reunification would be much more difficult without his guidance. So, much time was spent in talking about Lincoln's death that the subject of Johnston's surrender was hardly broached. Accordingly, the two commanders agreed to meet the following day at the same place to conclude the discussion of surrender.

At this second meeting, Sherman proposed terms that were magnanimous to Johnston's army. He also included nonmilitary items of a political nature that were not within his power to grant. In short, Cump had agreed to allow Johnston's men simply to return home, bearing their arms, which were to be deposited in their respective state arsenals. The legislatures of the Confederate states would be allowed to continue governing so long as they took an oath of allegiance to the United States. Federal courts were to be reestablished throughout the South. Inhabitants of the South would be guaranteed their rights of person and property, including the right to vote, regardless of their participation in the war. Sherman had declared a general amnesty for the citizens of the Confederacy, and proposed that the country be reunited with no recriminations or assessment of guilt. The principles signed the agreement, and when Sherman returned to his headquarters, in Raleigh, he wired news of the meeting to Secretary Stanton.

Stanton was outraged by the terms Cump had granted. He accused Sherman of treason for the way he had meddled in political issues that were beyond his authority and intimated that the general sought to set himself up as a dictator at the head of his army. President Andrew Johnson flatly refused to accept the document, and General Grant was summoned to the White House. Grant was instructed to proceed to North Carolina to personally take charge of Sherman's army. He was to offer Johnston the same terms that Lee had been given at Appomattox, and if these were declined, he was to move upon the Army of the South with all dispatch. In the meantime, Stanton leaked the story to the press, intimating that Sherman had been bribed by Confederates to allow Jefferson Davis to escape through his lines with the South's treasury. Northern newspapers printed the allegations of Cump's treachery far and wide, and Northern citizens cried out against the general with an outrage that equaled that of the people of Georgia and the Carolinas.

Sherman's career and reputation hung in the balance. Berated throughout the South as an arsonist and thief who had robbed and burned his way across three states, he was now on the verge of being relieved of command for showing too much leniency to the people of the Confederacy. All of his accomplishments were now forgotten, and Cump faced the prospect of being sent home in disgrace. Grant arrived at Sherman's headquarters on April 24, but he did not strictly follow his instructions from the president. "When I arrived I went to Sherman's headquarters, and we were at once closeted together. I showed him the instructions and orders under which I visited him. I told him that I wanted him to notify General Johnston that the terms which they had conditionally agreed upon had not been approved in Washington, and that he was authorized to offer the same terms I had given General Lee. I sent Sherman to do this himself. I did not wish the knowledge of my presence to be known to the army generally; so I left it to Sherman to negotiate the terms of surrender solely by himself, and without the enemy knowing that I was anywhere near the field. As soon as possible I started to get away, to leave Sherman quite free and untrammeled."

Sherman sent word of the developments to Johnston, informing him that the truce existing between the two armies would cease in 48 hours if Johnston refused to accept the terms. President Jefferson Davis, then in Charlotte, balked at agreeing to new terms. Johnston had experienced great difficulty in persuading the president to consent to Sherman's original terms, and now that they had been altered, Davis ordered Johnston to disband his army with instructions to reassemble at a later place and time. But Johnston disobeyed his superior. Convinced that it would be criminal to prolong the war any further, he

Bennett Place, North Carolina, where Sherman accepted the surrender of Gen. Joseph E. Johnston's Confederate Army. (U.S. Military History Institute)

wrote to Sherman, asking for a meeting between the two commanders. Johnston's message arrived at Sherman's headquarters on the morning of April 26, as the Federal troops were preparing to march against the Army of the South. Cump suggested that the meeting take place at the Bennett House at noon.

General Johnston argued that his army should get better terms than those offered to General Lee, owing to the difference in circumstances between the two armies. Lee's army had been completely surrounded by Grant at Appomattox Courthouse and had no options except capitulation or annihilation. Johnston's army still had choices available to it. The Army of the South had put a distance of 80 miles between itself and Sherman's army. It was not trapped or surrounded, and could escape into Georgia, to prolong the war. Sherman lent a deaf ear to Johnston's arguments. Restricted, as he was, to the terms offered by Lee's army, he could offer no concessions. In the end, Johnston agreed to the terms and the document of surrender was signed. When Cump returned to Raleigh, Grant endorsed the terms of surrender before departing for Washington. He had salvaged the reputation of his subordinate and

Sherman, as he appeared in 1865, at the end of the war. (U.S. Military History Institute)

friend by allowing him to broker the capitulation of Johnston's army under terms the government would accept.

The surrender of Johnston's army brought a close to the Civil War. Although there were numerous small bands of Confederate soldiers still in the field, the Confederacy had ceased to exist with the elimination of its last real army. Sherman had been as responsible as any officer in the Union army for the defeat of the Confederacy, and now, because of Grant, he would be able to preserve his reputation and receive the accolades his accomplishments deserved.

Chapter 13

THE FINAL COMMANDS

The end of the war brought with it many questions as to how the former Confederate states would be brought back into the Union. President Lincoln had favored a policy of lenient measures, advocating that the South be let up easy, but the president was now dead, and radical faction of his party had taken control of the government. Andrew Johnson, Stanton, and others of the radical mind-set favored a system of reconstruction that would punish the South, and cried out against terms that had already been ratified, preventing the execution of leaders like Robert E. Lee and Joe Johnston for treason. Sherman observed this change of sentiment within the government with horror. To be sure, he had proven himself a scourge of the South, and the burnt earth tactics of his last two campaigns had brought the Confederacy to its knees, but that was war. His objective had been to bring the war to a close in the fastest possible manner, and Cump felt that the cruelty of his campaigns would be the shortest way to victory and an end to the bloodshed. He genuinely liked Southerners and supported Lincoln's policies regarding the readmission of the Confederate states into the Union. The retribution and recrimination sought by the Johnson administration seemed criminal to him. In a letter to his wife, Sherman

wrote that the "suffering coming to the South will be beyond compre-
hension. People who talk of further retaliation and punishment, except of political leaders, either do not conceive the suffering endured
already, or they are heartless or unfeeling."

On May 10, President Davis was captured at Irwinville, Georgia
in one of the final chapters of the war. With the Confederate armies
surrendered and disbanded, and the most prominent member of the
Confederate government in captivity, the nation was now prepared to
celebrate the conclusion of the war. President Johnson declared that the
rebellion and armed resistance was virtually at an end and decreed that
a review of the national troops take place in Washington prior to their
being mustered out of the service. The Army of the Potomac was already
at the capital when Sherman arrived with his Army of Georgia in the
middle of May. Sherman's force, along with the Army of the Tennessee,
was camped across the Potomac River from the army that bore its name,
but there was frequent contact between the eastern and western troops.
Troops from the Army of the Potomac looked down upon the westerners
as being undisciplined and slovenly in their appearance, and the westerners thought their eastern compatriots to paper collar dandies who
did not know how to fight. North had just defeated South, but now East
battled West in a multitude of fistfights and brawls that erupted in the
taverns, brothels, and along the streets of Washington.

On May 23, the Army of the Potomac marched down Pennsylvania
Avenue, past a reviewing stand in front of the White House. President
Johnson, General Grant, members of the Cabinet, and other political
dignitaries watched as Gen. George G. Meade led the 80,000 troops
of the Army of the Potomac in review. Marching 12 men abreast, the
massed columns filled the streets, and took over six hours to file past
the dignitaries and throngs of cheering citizens who lined the way. On
May 24, it was Sherman's turn to march in review. For the people of
Washington, this was the main event of the celebration. The Army of
the Potomac had operated in close proximity to Washington, and its
men and leaders were well known within the capital. Sherman's western armies were a novelty within the city. Most had never before seen
these victors of Shiloh, Chickamauga, Atlanta, and Nashville. Sherman himself was a curiosity to most of the citizens of the city who had

never before laid eyes on him. Cump had anticipated that his armies would be the center of attention and fretted they would not present themselves in a proper manner. Sherman had trained his men to fight and had paid little attention to many of the subtleties of military discipline. For several days, prior to the review, he had his officers put the men through rigorous sessions of close order drill to ensure they did not embarrass themselves while marching through the city. But he need not have been worried. The 65,000 men of his command performed splendidly, receiving the accolades of the thankful residents of Washington for six hours as they marched in review through the city. Sherman led the troops, and when he reached the reviewing stand he stopped to acknowledge those present. Although he greeted President Johnson, General Grant, and several of other dignitaries there, he refused contact with Stanton, delivering a public snub viewed by all in attendance. Stanton's efforts to besmirch Cump's reputation would not soon be forgotten by the general.

On May 30, Sherman officially bid farewell to the soldiers who had fought by his side for four long years as he took his leave from the army

The Grand Review of Sherman's western army, held in Washington, DC, on May 24, 1865. (U.S. Military History Institute)

prior to its disbandment. In a touching address, he told them, "The General commanding announces to the Armies of the Tennessee and Georgia that the time has come for us to part. Our work is done, and armed enemies no longer defy us. Some of you will go to your homes, and others will be retained in military service until further orders." After praising their service and highlighting their victories, Cump said, "Your General now bids you farewell, with the full belief that, as in war you have been good soldiers, so in peace you will make good citizens."

Following his departure from the army, Sherman accompanied his family to Chicago to lend his assistance to a fair held for the purpose of raising money to aid impoverished soldiers' families, before taking a leave to visit Lancaster, Louisville, and Nashville. On June 27, 1865, he was placed in command of the Military Division of the Mississippi, but was later shifted to command of the Military Division of the Missouri, with headquarters at St. Louis. This posting gave Cump great satisfaction, as it meant that he would be able to supervise a portion of the construction of the trans-continental railroad. Sherman had been a proponent of a rail line that linked east to west from long before the Civil War. He had urged his brother to push for legislation in Congress to make the railroad a reality, saying that he would gladly give his life to see the project successfully completed, as he felt it would do wonders toward unifying the country. Now, he was to command the military division in which a large portion of the railroad was to be built, and it was with great joy that he witnessed the Union Pacific Railroad laying track westward from Omaha, Nebraska.

The mustering out of the Federal armies necessitated many changes in the organizational structure of the U.S. Army. When Ulysses S. Grant was promoted to the rank of full general on July 25, 1865, Sherman was promoted to fill the now voided rank of lieutenant general. Other offers of promotion were soon to come Cump's way. President Johnson had broken with the Republican Party over disputes dealing with reconstruction of the Southern states. He now found himself in open warfare against the radical faction of the party, championed by his own secretary of war, Edwin Stanton. Johnson sought to oust Stanton from office, and asked for his resignation. Stanton declined. Johnson then removed Stanton, appointing General Grant to temporarily take his place. This action was in violation of the newly passed Tenure of Office Act that Congress had voted into law over Johnson's veto. The law provided for prison terms and hefty fines for any person violating its provisions. Upon learning of these provisions, Grant determined to resign his temporary position as secretary of war. Johnson then offered the cabinet office to Sherman. He hoped to enlist Cump's support in his battle against the radicals, but Sherman wanted nothing to do with the political intrigue. Though he favored Johnson's policies toward the South, he still detested politics and wished to have nothing to do with becoming part of the government.

Johnson next tried to create the appearance of support from Sherman by naming him commander of the Military Division of the Atlantic, headquartered in Washington. Cump was well known to be lenient in his feelings for the defeated Southerners and opposed to immediate Negro suffrage. Johnson felt that Cump's presence in the capital would serve as an endorsement of his own more lenient attitude toward the South. Sherman declined this offer as well. He had no desire to live in Washington amid the swirling intrigues of the politicians, and he was not about to allow himself to be unwittingly cast into the fight. He turned down the assignment and hinted that he was fully prepared to resign from the army if compelled to accept it.

Back in St. Louis, Sherman devoted his time to overseeing the construction of the trans-continental railroad. The major concern confronting the project was its periodic interruption by bands of warring Indians. Cump showed his contradictory nature to its fullest when it came to his dealings with the Indians of the plains. He personally felt a great deal of sympathy for the tribes and empathized with them over the encroachment of whites into their lands and the treacherous manner in which they had been dealt with by the government. In August 1866 he would write Grant that the Indians in his military division were "pure beggars and poor devils more to be pitied than dreaded." He informed his superior that a great many Indian outrages had been precipitated by whites who hoped that his troops would wipe out the red race. "I will not permit them to be warred against as long as they are not banded together in parties large enough to carry on war," he assured Grant. By December, he had changed his opinion. A massacre of soldiers prompted him to write Grant, "We must act with vindictive earnestness against the Sioux, even to their extermination, men, women and children." His response was comparable to the course he had adopted in Georgia two years before. He was sympathetic toward the Indians, just as he had been toward Southerners, but believed that only iron-fisted measures could put down insurrection and rebellion against the authority of the government. With Sherman, there was no conflict between his personal sympathies and his professional actions. It was his duty to enforce the rule of the government.

In September 1867, Sherman headed a peace commission charged by the administration with brokering a treaty with several of the plains tribes. The conference was held at Fort Laramie, Wyoming. Cump advised the Indians that they should stake claim to their homes before all of the good land had been taken by whites and urged them to adapt to reservation life. Although the conference showed little initial success, it laid the groundwork for triumph. By 1872 Sherman could boast that he had been responsible for seeing the Navahoes, Cheyennes, Kiowas, Arapahoes, and Comanches all settled into reservation life. Following the defeat of Col. George Armstrong Custer's Seventh Cavalry at the Little Big Horn Sherman once more assumed a punitive attitude toward the warring tribes. He wrote that "hostile savages like Sitting Bull and his band of outlaw Sioux . . . must feel the superior power of the Government." He also stated that "during an assault, the soldiers can not pause to distinguish between male and female, or even discriminate as to age." As soon as the uprising was put down, Cump went back to advocating for Indian rights and speaking out against unfair practices of government agents against them.

The year 1867 also witnessed the enlargement of the Sherman family with the birth of Philemon Tecumseh Sherman on January 9. His growing family caused Cump to despair over his ability to financially support the Sherman brood. Cump was generous to a fault and often donated sums of money to soldier's relief groups. He and Ellen maintained an active social calendar, attending many parties and balls. As was the custom of the times, guests at any social event were then expected to host a similar event, and that cost money. While Sherman's pay as a lieutenant general was more than adequate to provide a comfortable lifestyle for his family, it proved insufficient to live in the manner Cump felt his rank and station demanded.

By 1868 it had become evident that Ulysses S. Grant would become the next president of the United States. Sherman had hoped that his old friend would steer clear of politics, but the enthusiasm sweeping the greatest Union hero of the war toward the nation's highest office was resistless. Grant was elected in a landslide, and when he was sworn in on March 4, 1869, Sherman was elevated to the rank of full general and appointed general of the army. Phil Sheridan was promoted to lieutenant general to replace Sherman, much to the chagrin of Gen. George Thomas. Sherman tried to soothe his old friend and West Point classmate by offering him his choice of departments. Thomas selected the Department of the Pacific, with headquarters in San Francisco.

Cump's promotion to full general was something of a mixed reward. Although the rank showed the appreciation of the government for his many and varied services to the country, it also meant that he would have to reside in Washington, amid all of the political entanglements of the day. Ellen was elated over the promotion. It would mean that she

Sherman as full general of the U.S. Army. Note the disappearance of the wrinkles and care-worn appearance that had so defined the general's face at the conclusion of the war. (U.S. Military History Institute)

would be able to be close to family members residing in the city. Cump worried about his ability to afford life in Washington, but that fear was removed when a group of influential supporters raised the money to purchase the house Grant had been living in and presented it to Sherman as a gift.

One would have thought that there would be a harmonious relationship between Grant and Sherman as commander in chief and general of the army, but such was not the case. Although Cump's loyalty to Grant was never questioned, he objected to the way in which Grant was manipulated by radical members of the Republican Party. Sherman felt that Grant had surrounded himself with a low class of men and was particularly scathing in his assessment of John Rawlins, a former member of Grant's staff and now his secretary of war. Under Rawlins's direction, much of the authority of the general of the army was transferred to the war department. When Cump complained to Grant that he was being stripped of his ability to command the army the president begged off any intercession between his two friends by stating that Rawlins was terribly ill and he did not wish to upset his condition. Rawlins was indeed ill. He was in the final stages of tuberculosis, and the disease would claim his life on September 6, 1869.

Upon the death of Rawlins, Grant requested Sherman to assume the responsibilities of interim secretary of war until a replacement could be found. From September 7 till October 25, Cump performed the dual duties of general of the army and secretary of war. At Cump's urging, Grant selected William W. Belknap, of Iowa, as his next secretary of war. Belknap had served under Sherman in the western army, and had left a favorable impression on his old commander. But bravery on the battlefield did not translate to character in political office, as Cump later discovered, much to his chagrin. Belknap proved to be one of the most corrupt members of Grant's cabinet, and would later hold the distinction of being the only cabinet secretary to be impeached by the House of Representatives.

Sherman detested the politics of Washington, and by 1871, was ready to take his leave of the capital. When Admiral James Alden told him he was sailing to Europe on navy business and offered to take him along for a tour of the continent, Cump jumped at the opportunity. In early November, he took a leave of absence from the army a set sail for a 10-month tour of Europe and the Middle East. Cump made this voyage by himself. Neither Ellen nor any of the children accompanied him. His travels took him to Spain, Italy, Turkey, Egypt, Russia, Switzerland, Germany, France, and Great Britain. Although he traveled as a common tourist, his fame and celebrity status met him at every stop. Everywhere he was treated to dinners and receptions in his honor.

When Sherman returned home on September 22, 1872, it was to find Grant almost certain of being reelected. Politicians in Washington were already looking ahead to the next presidential contest, in 1876, and Sherman found himself their leading candidate for consideration. In no uncertain terms, the general made it known that he had no interest in attaining political office and would turn down a nomination should it come his way. His financial situation became acute following his return from the European trip. Taxes on his home rose from $400 per year to $1,500, prompting him to move the family into half the house and rent the other half out to meet expenses. In 1874, Cump moved the family to St Louis, to escape both the high cost of living in Washington as well as the political bureaucrats. St. Louis became the headquarters of the army, and many in Washington gossiped that Cump had quit the city because he was too honest to stand the corruption of Grant's administration.

Life was easier for the Shermans in St. Louis. Cump had time to devote to his memoirs, which he had begun earlier that same year. By the end of 1874 he had completed his manuscript, but feared having them published "lest it should involve me in personal controversies." Overcoming his fears, he sent the manuscript to D. Appleton & Co. of New York. The publisher was anxious to put the memoirs into print. Sherman was the first of the major commander of the war to publish his memoirs, and as such, the book was groundbreaking in the history of the war. Published in two volumes, it quickly became the book of the year, as throngs of veterans purchased it to read the general's own words concerning his famous campaigns. The work received favorable reviews, but it was attacked by supporters of the Army of the Cumberland and officers like George Thomas, Don Carlos Buell, William S. Rosecrans, and others that the supporters felt to be slighted by Sherman. Cump admitted that he might have made some errors in the text

and was mortified at the charge that he had been unjust to fellow officers and friends like Thomas, Schofield, and McPherson. He offered
to make corrections to the book for a reprinted edition, but was dis-
couraged from such by family and friends. The most profound effect of
Sherman's memoirs was that they reopened old wounds for the people
of the South. Cump had been generally well thought of in the former
Confederacy, but his frank and open history of the campaigns that had
so demoralized the South caused him once more to be hated as a focal
point in the "Lost Cause" mentality that was developing.

Toward the end of 1875 there was a resurgence of support for Sherman becoming the Republican candidate for the next presidential election. He flatly refused. Grant's administration was riddled with graft
and corruption, and Republican leaders were seeking a candidate whose
honest reputation could offset the patronage and greed that seemed everywhere in the present government. Secretary Belknap resigned his
position at the war department in March owing to a scandal for selling
butlership to army posts to the highest bidder. The removal of Belknap
required that Sherman relocate to Washington to conduct his affairs
with the army. His arrival in the capital was with great reluctance, but
it could not have been at a better time.

The election of 1876 proved to be one of the most closely contested
and controversial in American history. Rutherford B. Hayes ran on the
Republican ticket against the Democratic candidate, John Tilden. The
results were so close that a winner could not be determined. Neither
candidate had the 185 electoral votes necessary to become president,
and the 25 electoral votes from Oregon, South Carolina, Florida, and
Louisiana were being disputed and were up for grabs. The government
never before had to deal with a disputed election, and the Constitution made had no provisions for the event, so it was decided that a
commission of representatives from the House of Representatives, the
Senate, and the Supreme Court should decide the winner in each of
the disputed states. The commission worked from November 8, 1876,
until March 2, 1877, to come up with its decision. In the end, the commission ruled on the disputed states along party lines. The eight Republican members outvoted their seven Democratic comrades to award
Hayes's 185 electoral votes to Tilden's 184. Both parties claimed that
they had been cheated in the decision, and threats of violence were

common as the sides squared off to protect their own interests. Sherman was equal to the challenge. He stationed troops throughout the city and vowed to shoot down anyone causing trouble or civil unrest, regardless of their party affiliation. To Sherman, this was politics at its worst. "If civil war breaks out," he wrote, "it will be a thousand times worse than the other war. It will be the fighting of neighbor against neighbor, friend against friend . . . There is only a question of time until the politicians ruin us. Partisanship is a curse. These men are not howling for the country's good but for their own political advantage and the people are too big fools to see it." It is impossible to know how much Sherman's strong stance influenced events in Washington, but the inauguration of Rutherford Hayes took place on March 5, just three days after the commission arrived at its decision, and there were no incidents to mar the occasion.

Cump's time in Washington during Hayes's administration was more pleasant than he anticipated. Both the president and his wife were huge fans of Sherman, and Hayes deferred to him on a variety of military issues. Most of the authority that had been stripped from Sherman

Sherman as he appeared in 1876. (U.S. Military History Institute)

during Belknap's time as secretary of war was returned. Cump spent a great deal of time, during this period, attending conventions and conferences for veterans' societies. He was a member of the Grand Army of the Republic, but took no leading role in its functions and activities. The G.A.R. was a highly political organization, firmly aligned with the Republican Party, and this was repugnant to Sherman. For him, politics had no business in a soldier's society, and the fact that the G.A.R. often targeted brother officers because of their Democratic affiliation caused him to steer clear of many of their events. The Society of the Army of the Tennessee became his pet veteran's group, in part because its members were the nearest and dearest to his heart, and in part because the society refused to embroil itself in politics. Sherman gave many speeches to gatherings of the society, amid the cheers of men who had once followed him in his march through the South.

In 1879, Sherman delivered a speech to the graduating class of the Michigan Military Academy in which he possibly uttered the famous "War is Hell" phrase that has come to be so closely associated with his name. It is definite that he made reference to it on April 11, 1880, during a speech given at Columbus, Ohio. "There is many a boy here today who looks on war as all glory," he had said, "but boys, it is all hell."

By 1882, Sherman was beginning to think of leaving the army. That year, Congress passed a law mandating that soldiers and officers in the army be retired at the age of 64. Cump was 63 and would reach the mandatory age on his next birthday. Although he was assured that an exception to the law would be made on his behalf, Cump refused to accept any preferential treatment. He felt that a good commander must abide by the same regulations that governed his officers and men. Accordingly, Sherman submitted his resignation as general of the army on November 1, 1883. Phil Sheridan was promoted to replace him. On February 8, 1884, Cump asked that his name be placed on the retired list, as he took his leave from the army.

Private life did not remove the general from the affairs of state. As soon as his resignation was accepted politicians began to once more call for his candidacy in the next presidential election. Cump did his best to stifle these political designs, but with no clear alternative candidate, party leaders kept coming back to Sherman. At the Republican convention, held at Chicago in June of 1884, delegates were divided among several candidates. Cump received a wire from one of the delegates informing him, "Your name is the only one we can agree upon, you will have to put aside your prejudices and accept the Presidency." Sherman's response left little room for doubt. "I will not accept if nominated and will not serve if elected."

In many ways, Sherman did not have time to be president. Always in demand as a speaker, he received an invitation per day following his retirement. His presence at these functions was not merely due to his status as a celebrity. Cump was acknowledged to be one of the finest dinner orators of his time. About two years after his retirement, the Shermans relocated to New York City. For the first couple of years they resided in a hotel before buying a house at 75 West 71st Street. Cump availed himself of his passion for the theater by attending many of the best openings in the city, and he accepted numerous invitations to speak.

Cump's life of ease and leisure was broken for a time by the death of his longtime friend and comrade, Ulysses S. Grant. On July 23, 1885, Grant lost his final battle to throat cancer, approximately a week after finishing his own memoirs of the war. Sherman was shocked and saddened by Grant's death, even though he knew the old general's passing was eminent. Indeed, it had only been through Grant's dogged willpower that he had been able to live that long. Penniless and with his family facing the prospects of a life of destitution, Grant fought off the reaper's hand as he struggled to finish the manuscript of his wartime recollections that he hoped would result in financial security for his wife and children. Although he attended Grant's funeral, he did not speak. Credited as being one of the most capable orators in the land, he could not find the words to convey his sense of loss and sorrow.

On November 28, 1888, Cump was forced to face the reality of being alone when Ellen died. Suffering from an affliction of the heart for several years, she had been reduced to being an invalid by the time the Shermans had moved into their house on 71st Street. Cump had tried to encourage her by saying that her father had suffered from the same affliction for many years and that she was in no danger of dying. But Ellen's condition continued to worsen, and for the last weeks of her life she was confined to her bed, under the care of a full-time nurse. Cump continued to convince himself that Ellen would rally, however, until the moment came when the nurse announced she was dying. He ran to her bedside an instant before she breathed her last, at 9:30 A.M. in the morning. After the funeral service, Cump accompanied her body to St. Louis. The couple had previously discussed their burial plans and had decided that their final resting place should be in Calvary Cemetery, beside Willie and their baby, Charles.

Friends and family kept the general active and engaged, as did his busy schedule of speaking. Veterans' groups continued to be close to his heart, and he devoted a great deal of time to the affairs of his old soldiers. After observing his 70th birthday, contemporaries felt that he experienced a distraction in his mental abilities and frequently drifted from his well-known realism into bouts of sentimentality and romantic reflection. It may be that Cump was coming to grips with his own mortality and was trying to evaluate his life and accomplishments in terms that went beyond the facts and figures of the historical record. Sixteen guests had been invited to his home to help him celebrate his 70th birthday, including such notable military comrades as John Schofield, Henry Slocum, and Oliver O. Howard. Howard had stated that "Sherman will never die." Cump responded by telling those gathered, "I am too old to hope for many returns of the day . . . Death seems to come nowadays without almost any warning, but many a man sprang up in readiness when I have had the trumpets sounded, and I am still a soldier. When Gabriel sounds his trumpet I shall be ready."

Continual bouts of asthma prompted the general to prepare for his own death. Confiding to a niece, he said, "When I come home these nights, I feel as if Death walked with me and laid his hand upon my shoulder." Sherman left instructions that his funeral was to be a simple military affair. He wanted no exhibitions of his body in various cities, no "lying in state," and no ornate tomb of mausoleum. His request was to be buried beside his wife and sons, with a simple gravestone to mark his plot. He had even drawn an example of the tombstone he wanted, directing that it be inscribed simply with the epitaph, "William Tecumseh Sherman. General U.S.A. Born at Lancaster, O., Feb. 8, 1820. Died at ____ ____ ____. Faithful and Honorable."

On the evening of February 4, 1891, Sherman was returning home from a night at the theater in bitter cold weather. The next morning he awoke with a cold. Although ill and infirm, he attended a wedding that day, against the wishes of his children. By February 7, his condition had worsened, and doctors announced that he was suffering from facial erysipelas, a bacterial infection of the upper dermis and superficial lymphatics. February 8 was the general's birthday, but there was little to celebrate. A wire was sent to his son Thomas, a Catholic priest, attending a Jesuit seminary on the Island of Jersey that his father's condition was serious and he should return home with all possible haste. By February 12, Cump's condition had deteriorated to the point that a public announcement was made. Newspaper men crowded at the front door and lined the street in front of the Sherman house waiting to get the latest news on the nation's greatest living soldier. When Catholic priests entered the home to give extreme unction to the general, the reporters were quick to protest that last rites had been administered to Cump without his knowing, asserting that Sherman was not Catholic and disapproved of the priesthood, even though one of his sons had chosen that path in life. John Sherman attempted to set the matter right by stating that his brother was "too human a man to deny to his children the consolation of their religion. . . . He was insensible, but had he been in the full exercise of his faculties he would not have denied them. Certainly if I had been present I would have assented to and reverently shared in an appeal to the Almighty for a life here and hereafter for my brother."

On the afternoon of February 12, Cump seemed to rally and even found the strength to get out of bed and sit in a chair for a while. John was so encouraged by his actions that he wired President Benjamin Harrison that there was a chance of his recovery. Indeed, the erysipelas seemed to be subsiding on February 13, and the general had been able to talk with family and friends, but the illness had left the general's body in a much weakened state. A severe bout of asthma, his old nemesis, set in and finally brought about his death at 1:50 P.M., on February 14, 1891.

Sherman's body was prepared by morticians, but it remained at his home for five days, waiting for his son Tom to arrive from overseas. On February 18, his family violated one of his wishes when the house was opened and thousands of mourners were allowed to come inside and file past his remains. He was dressed in his general's uniform, with a yellow sash across his breast, and his cap and sword lay upon the

Sherman as he appeared in the later years of his life, just prior to retirement. (U.S. Military History Institute)

coffin. Although Cump had desired no public viewing, his family felt that they could not deny so many veterans a last opportunity to pay tribute to their fallen commander. Weeping old soldiers shuffled by the casket, looking for the last time upon the face of the commander they had followed through four long years of war, amid the muffled utterances of Shiloh, Vicksburg, and Atlanta. Tom arrived on the afternoon of February 19 and was taken by his sisters to his father's casket. He wept uncontrollably at the sight of his father's face, but was able to regain his composure sufficiently to perform the funeral service later the same day.

The city of New York was in mourning. Flags were at half-mast throughout the city and on ships in the harbor. Some 30,000 members of the National Guard, West Point cadets, and veterans assembled to escort his body from his home to a ferry boat that would transport the coffin to a waiting train that would bear it directly to St. Louis. The flag-draped casket was carried out of the house and placed on an artillery caisson. Close by was a horse with the general's saddle, his boots placed backward in the stirrups. President Harrison waited in a carriage behind the caisson, followed by ex-presidents Hayes and Cleveland, the Cabinet, and a host of congressmen, senators, governors, family, and friends. One of the honorary pallbearers was Gen. Joseph E. Johnston. Sherman's old antagonist was now 82 years old and in declining health himself. Despite this fact, the old warrior insisted on paying his respect by standing in the bitterly cold weather with his head uncovered as Sherman's body passed by. One of Johnston's attendants pleaded with him to put his hat on and protect himself from the cold, but the old general replied, "If I were in his place and he were standing here in mine, he would not put his hat on." Johnston would contact pneumonia from his final tribute, and it would claim his life a mere 10 days later.

The funeral procession marched through the streets of the city, lined with throngs of hushed and reverent citizens. When the body reached the railroad station it was placed in a funeral car. His picture was hung on the headlight of the engine, and his sword was hung below it. Cump's wishes not to have his body displayed in numerous cities en route to St. Louis was honored, but throngs of veterans and private citizens made their appearance to view the train and pay their respects as it passed westward along the line. In cities where the train was stopped for one reason or another, ex-soldiers were permitted to pass through the funeral car to view the closed coffin.

At St. Louis, another procession was held to accompany the casket from the funeral car to the burial site. Cump's son, Tom, performed a gravesite service, gathered veterans fired three volleys in tribute, and Taps was played. Sherman's body was lowered into the ground beside his cherished wife, and the crowd faded away. At a later date, the monument that Cump had designed himself was placed at his grave, and the soldier whose life was filled with so many great accomplishments and so many confounding contradictions was left to history's final deliberations.

AFTERWORD

William Tecumseh Sherman emerged from the Civil War as one of the most famous and iconic personalities in the country. He is generally acknowledged as being the first "modern general," and the manner in which he waged war influenced the actions of military leaders for generations to come. Above all, he was a soldier and viewed the complexities of war as a true professional of his craft. Although he truly liked Southerners, he did not hesitate to visit upon them war in its cruelest and most barbaric nature, confident that in doing so he could end the conflict sooner and bring about an end to the bloodshed. Responsible as much as any Northern leader for making the freeing of the slaves a reality, he clung to a belief that blacks were not yet ready to assimilate into mainstream society or serve as soldiers. Abolition was his pragmatic response to weakening the Confederate military, not an act of social conscious or reform. His aversion to politics, fostered during the 1840 presidential election, continued until his death, despite the fact that his family embraced the political arena and had risen to places of prominence. Three times, following the war, he had been approached to become the Republican candidate for president, and three times he had unequivocally refused. He had witnessed the unsavory side of politics and felt the profession beneath his honor and dignity. But he benefited greatly from his affiliations with his family as well as political supporters of noted friends, like Ulysses S. Grant. Indeed, much of Sherman's historical fame has been derived from the efforts of such men. His reputation was protected and enhanced by supporters of influence that were denied to other notable leaders like George H. Thomas.

While it can be argued that Sherman received recognition for accomplishments not fully of his own making, but his own record of achievement is indisputable. He had estimated the size and scope of the war long before most of his contemporaries. This insight had caused him to despair for the Union while in command in Kentucky and had led to his being relieved of command and branded as being insane. But time proved Cump to be all too correct in his prophecy. Along with Generals Prentiss and W.H.L. Wallace, he was responsible for holding the line at Shiloh, and not only preventing the destruction of Grant's army, but also of bleeding the enemy so profusely as to set the stage for victory on the following day. He handled his corps with skill at Vicksburg, sharing with Grant the fruits of the victory that opened the Mississippi River to flow unvexed to the sea. His Atlanta Campaign transferred the seat of war from Tennessee to the heart of Georgia, and his capture of that city filled war weary Northerners with hope and altered public opinion so dramatically that it changed Lincoln's prospects for reelection and snatched victory from the jaws of defeat. Cump's march through Georgia demonstrated to the people of the South that the war was lost in ways that no other campaign could have done, and his cruel tactics were successful in bringing the conflict to an early conclusion. The effects of his march through Georgia and the Carolinas were felt as far away as Virginia, where members of Robert E. Lee's Army of Northern Virginia deserted by the thousands in response to the forlorn letters of despair they received from family and loved ones left destitute by Sherman's path of destruction. His negotiations with General Johnston, resulting in the surrender of the Army of the South, helped to prevent the nation from being plunged into decades of guerrilla warfare and hatred that might have resulted if the terms of surrender had compelled the Confederates to disband and fight on. His conquest and occupation of vast portions of the Confederacy led to the emancipation of tens of thousands of slaves, and was as responsible as any action of the war to enforce President Lincoln's proclamation of freedom.

In the end, Sherman epitomized the highest standards of West Point in a life of loyalty, service, and dignity. Integrity of purpose and a fierce conviction for preserving order defined his military career, as well as his personal life. His hatred of sectional or political divisions among his countrymen caused him to put the nation's welfare above any other considerations as he fought for a unified America that was free from petty patronage and sectional disputes. For Sherman, it was the united in United States that mattered most, and his support for projects like the trans-continental railroad were based on his belief that the nation must be bound together to achieve its great potential as a leader in the world community. His campaigns forever changed the manner in which wars were fought and destroyed the myth of warfare being romantically heroic. War was hell, pure, and simple, and Cump had shown that fact to the world in unmistakable terms. But he had also shown that war did not have to breed continued animosity. His terms to Johnston's army and the consideration he extended to Johnston's troops helped to win the peace as much as his campaigns contributed to winning the war. It was this spirit that moved Joe Johnston to pay respect to a former enemy at the cost of his own life. It was a soldier's tribute, pure and simplistic, and was possibly the highest honor an officer of Sherman's character could have hoped for.

BIBLIOGRAPHICAL ESSAY

William T. Sherman has been written about in numerous books of a biographical nature, in works dealing with the history of the Civil War. In most cases, his biographers have endeavored to eulogize the man and promote his accomplishments in a manner intended to be more of a tribute than an accurate portrayal of history. This is especially true of early biographers, men who knew and admired the general. The work of more recent historians contains a balance not present in these earlier works and depicts a more rounded image of Sherman as the man and the general. This book has been compiled using a variety of sources, both modern and contemporary. Sherman's own words, contained in his two-volume work *The Memoirs of General William T. Sherman, by Himself*, provide the basis for his military experience, both in the Civil War and before. *Sherman and His Campaigns: A Military Biography* by S. M Bowman and R. B. Irwin was written in 1865, at a time when the events of the war were still fresh in the minds of those who experienced it. As such, it is filled with valuable information concerning Sherman's movements and leadership. *Life of Wm. Tecumseh Sherman, Late Retired General, U.S.A.*, by W. Fletcher Johnson, *Life and Deeds of General Sherman: Including the Story of His Great March to the Sea* by

Henry Davenport Northrop, and *The Life of General William T. Sherman* by James P. Boyd were all published in 1891, following Sherman's death, and were intended as tributes to the fallen commander. Even so, there is much good information to be found in each of these books. *Sherman: Fighting Prophet* by Lloyd Lewis was published in 1932. It was the first of the in-depth studies of Sherman's life and is possibly still the best. While it is evident that Lewis genuinely admires his subject and wishes to pay homage to his accomplishments, he does so in a manner that acknowledges Sherman's faults and shortcomings. *Sherman: A Soldier's Passion for Order*, written by John Marszalek, was published in 2007, and is one of the better modern biographies written about the general's life.

Other books of interest for the person wishing to read more about Sherman's life would include *Grant and Sherman: The Friendship That Won the Civil War* by Charles Bracelen Flood, *Sherman's March* by Burke Davis, *Marching Through Georgia* by Lee Kennett, *The Siege of Atlanta, 1864* by Samuel Carter III, *Worthy Opponents: William T. Sherman and Joseph E. Johnston: Antagonists in War-Friends in Peace* by Edward G. Longacre, and *Last Stand in the Carolinas: The Battle of Bentonville* by Mark L. Bradley. All of these books provide insight to the campaigns and relationships of Sherman presented in more in-depth manner than can usually be included in a one-volume biography. Many articles pertaining to Sherman and his campaigns can be found in the four-volume set *Battles and Leaders*, written by Sherman himself, as well as many of his contemporaries.

A wealth of information about Sherman can be found on the Internet, from his days in the California gold fields to his capture of Savannah. Most of the sites offer general information designed to inform and educate the reader. Every one of Sherman's campaigns has been written about extensively and can be found in great detail on the Internet. Certain websites and blogs, however, are still biased for or against Sherman, and their content is designed more to promote their bias than to provide balanced history. A basic knowledge of the war, and of Sherman's life, is necessary to cut through the propaganda in such places that generally go beyond the standard biographical essays.

INDEX

About the Author

ROBERT P. BROADWATER has written or contributed to 30 books on the American Revolution and the Civil War. He is the author of *Gettysburg as the Generals Remembered It: Postwar Perspectives of Ten Commanders* and *American Generals of the Revolutionary War: A Biographical Dictionary*. His published works also include more than 100 articles on military history, from the French and Indian War through World War II.